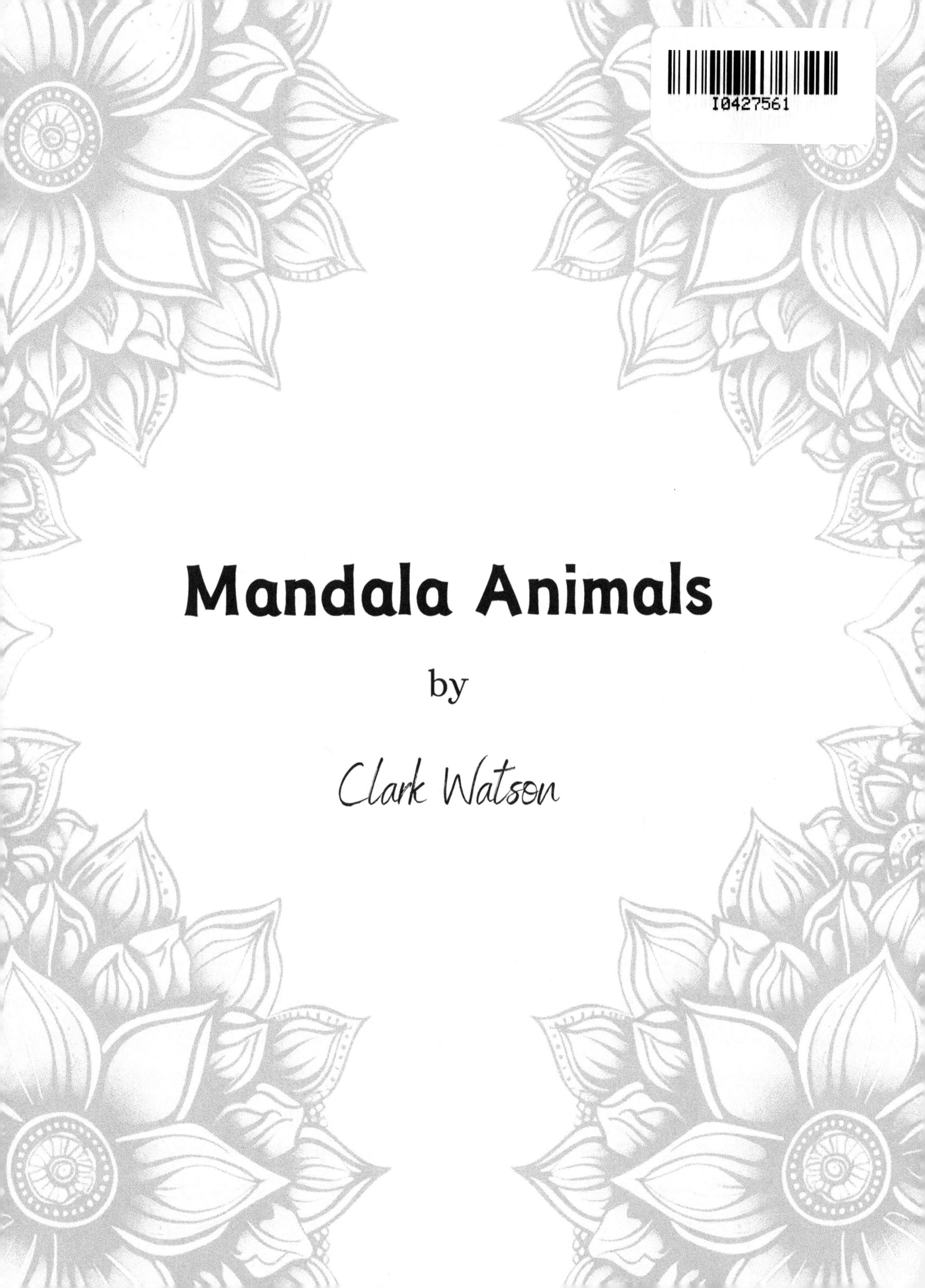

Mandala Animals

by

Clark Watson

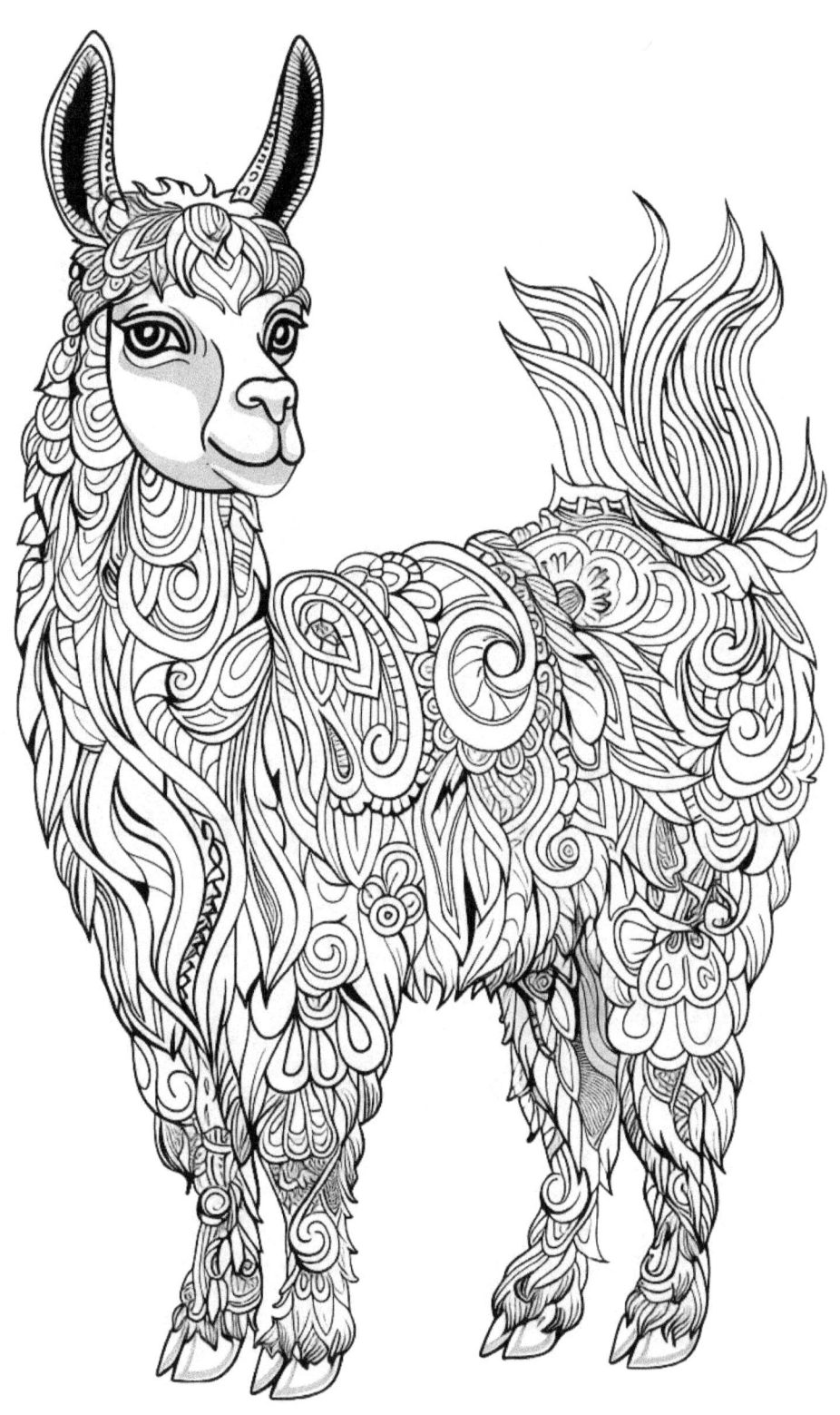

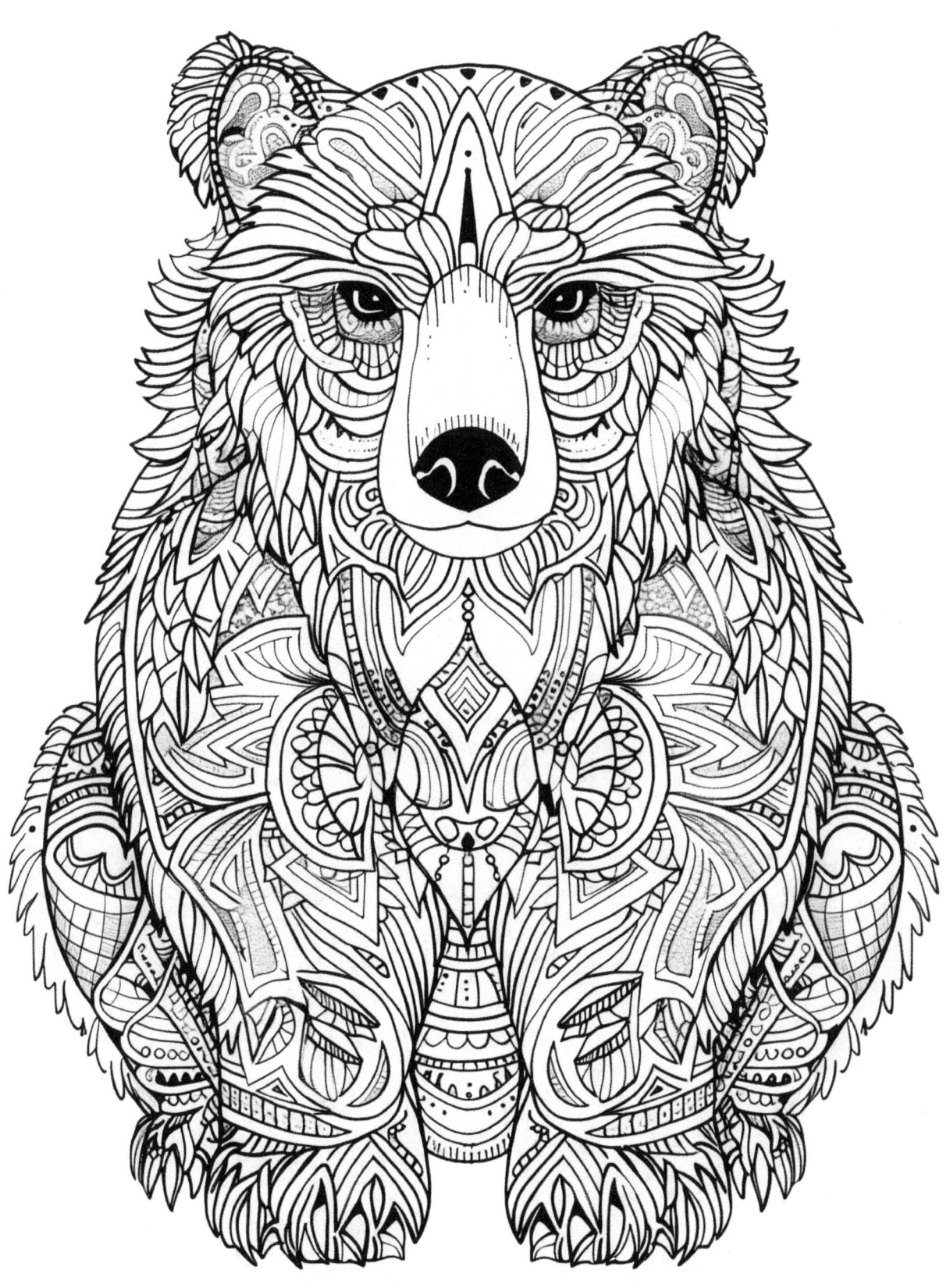

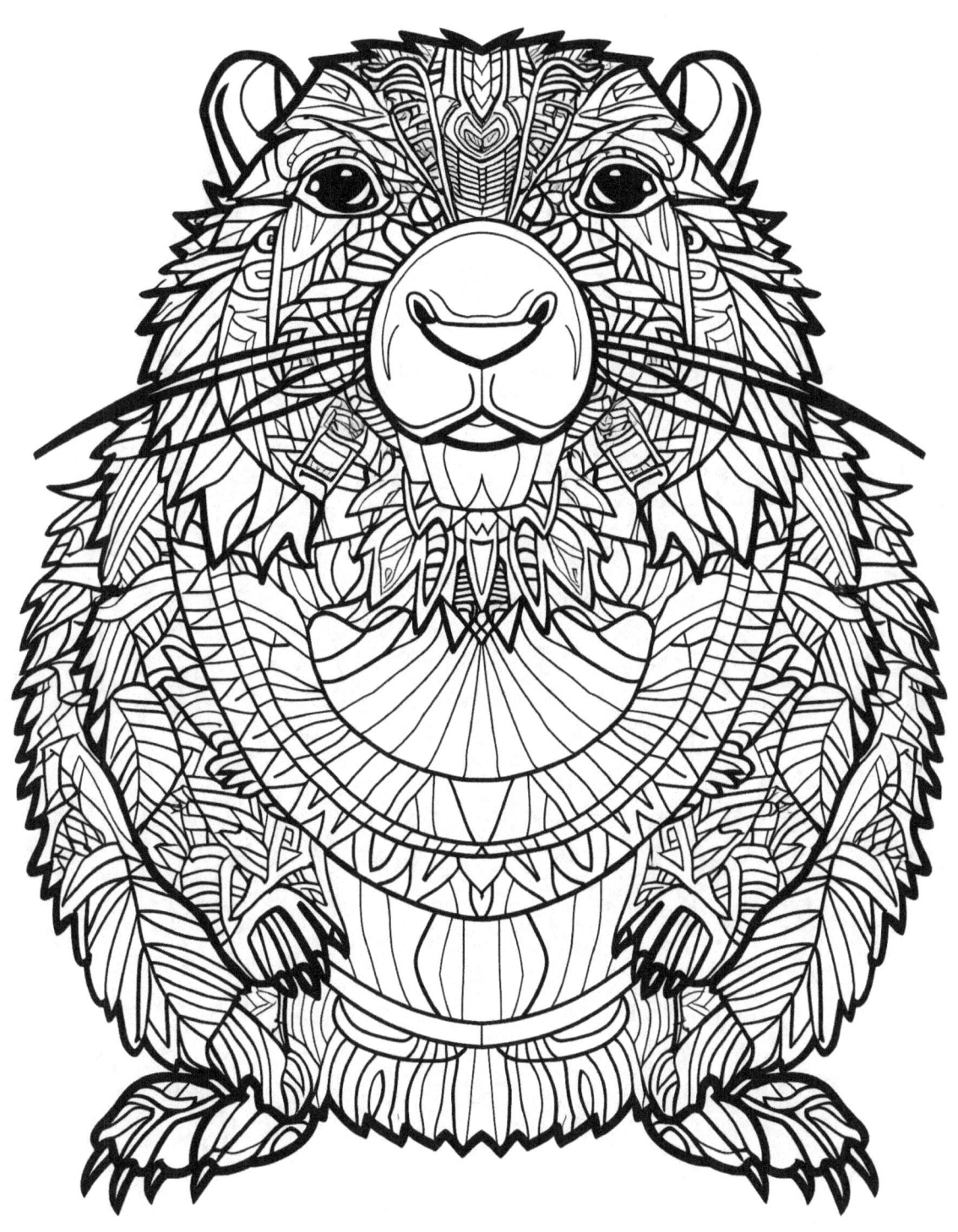

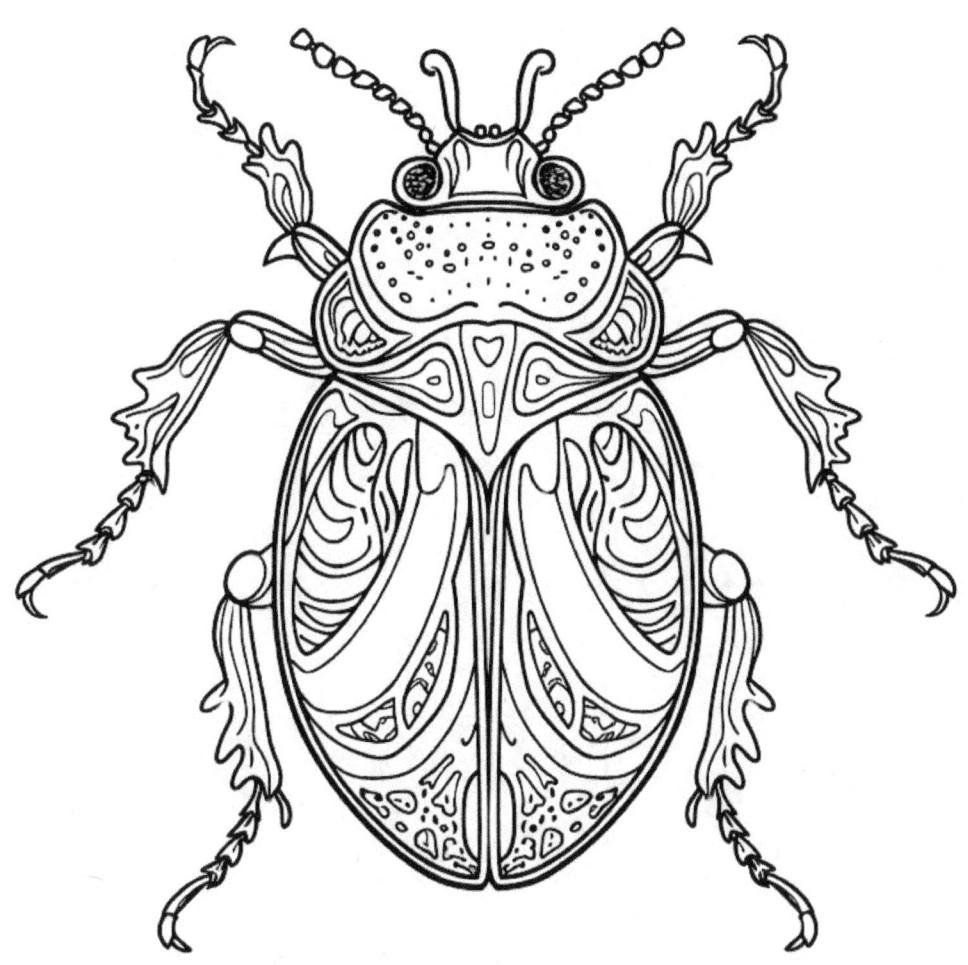

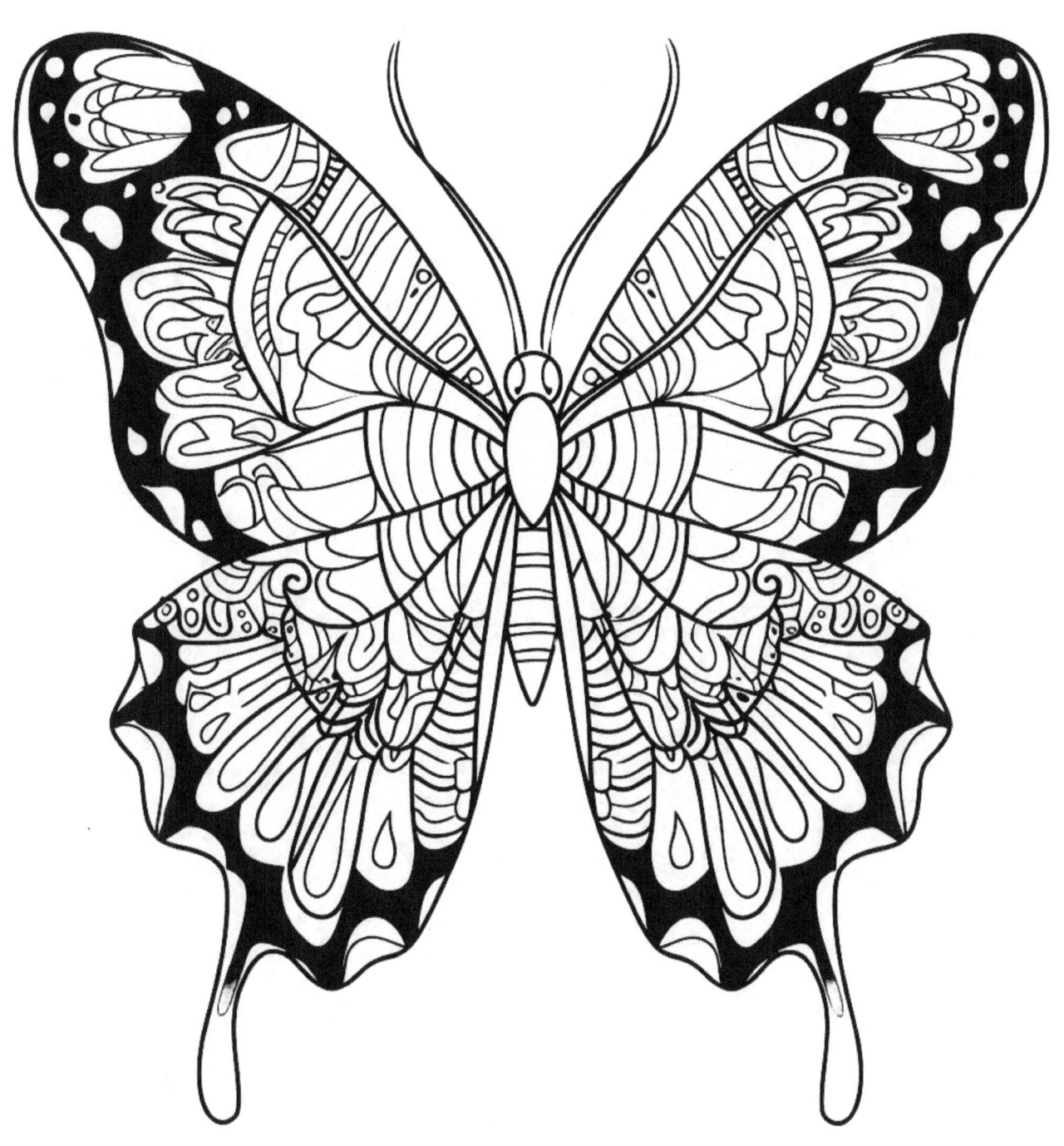

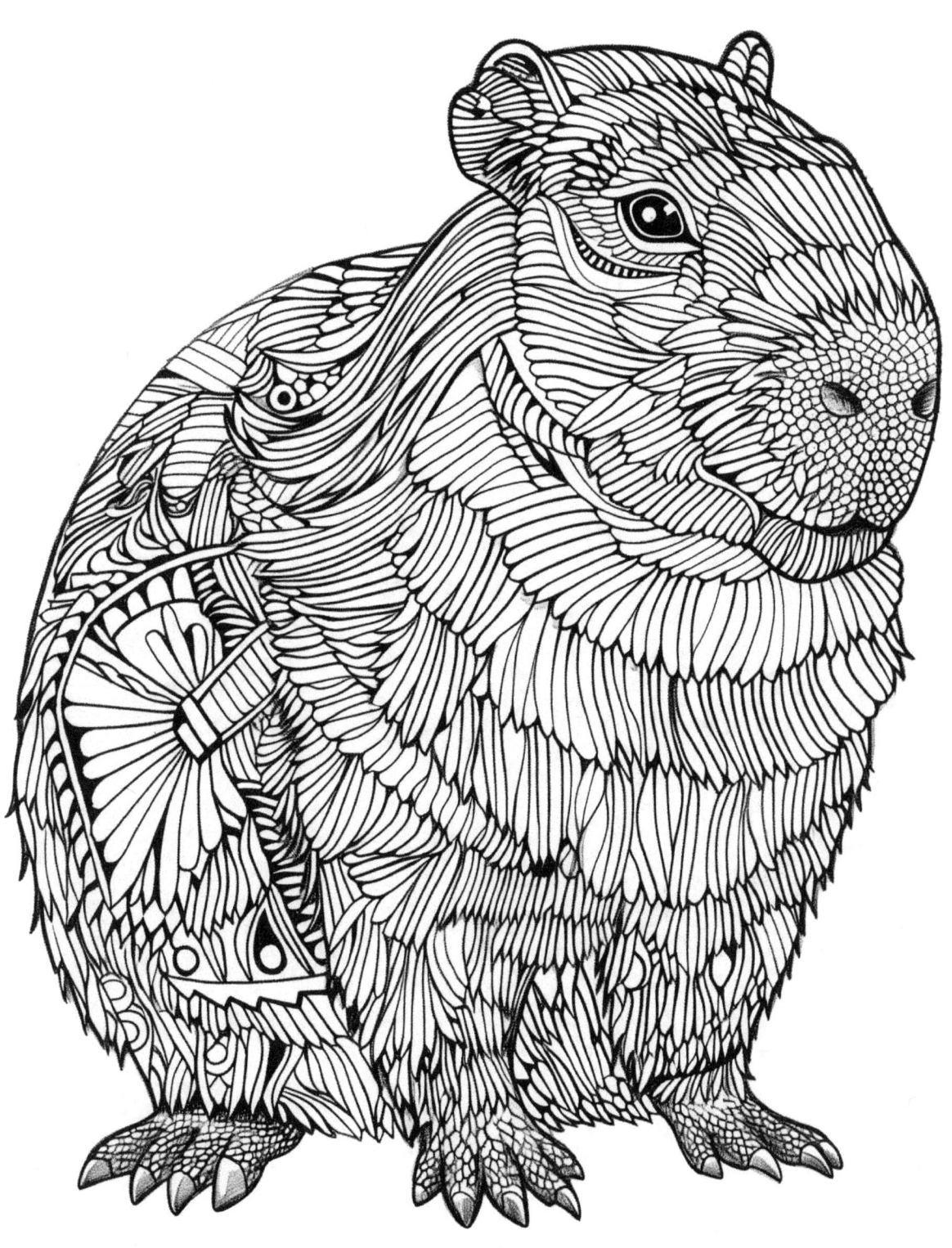

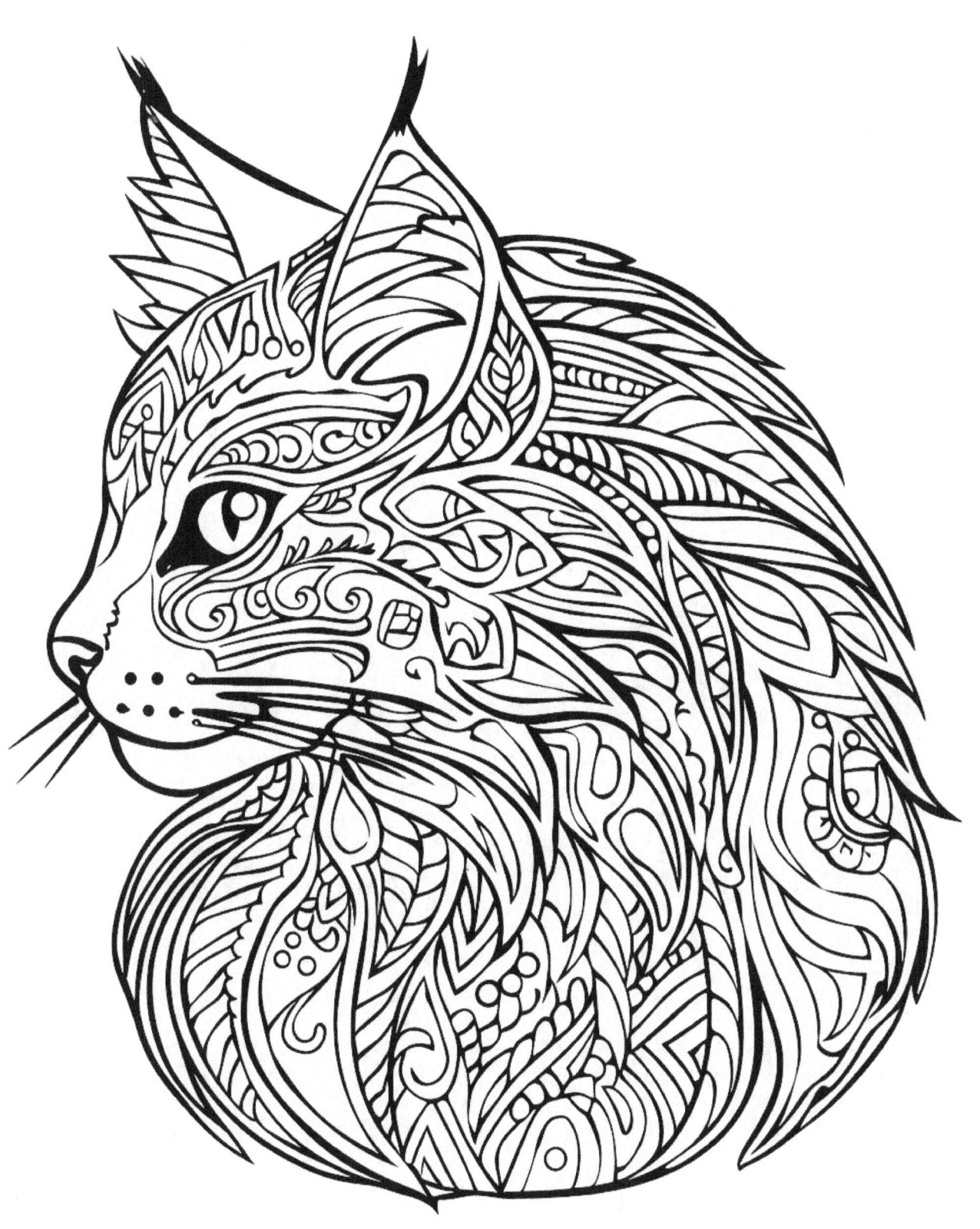

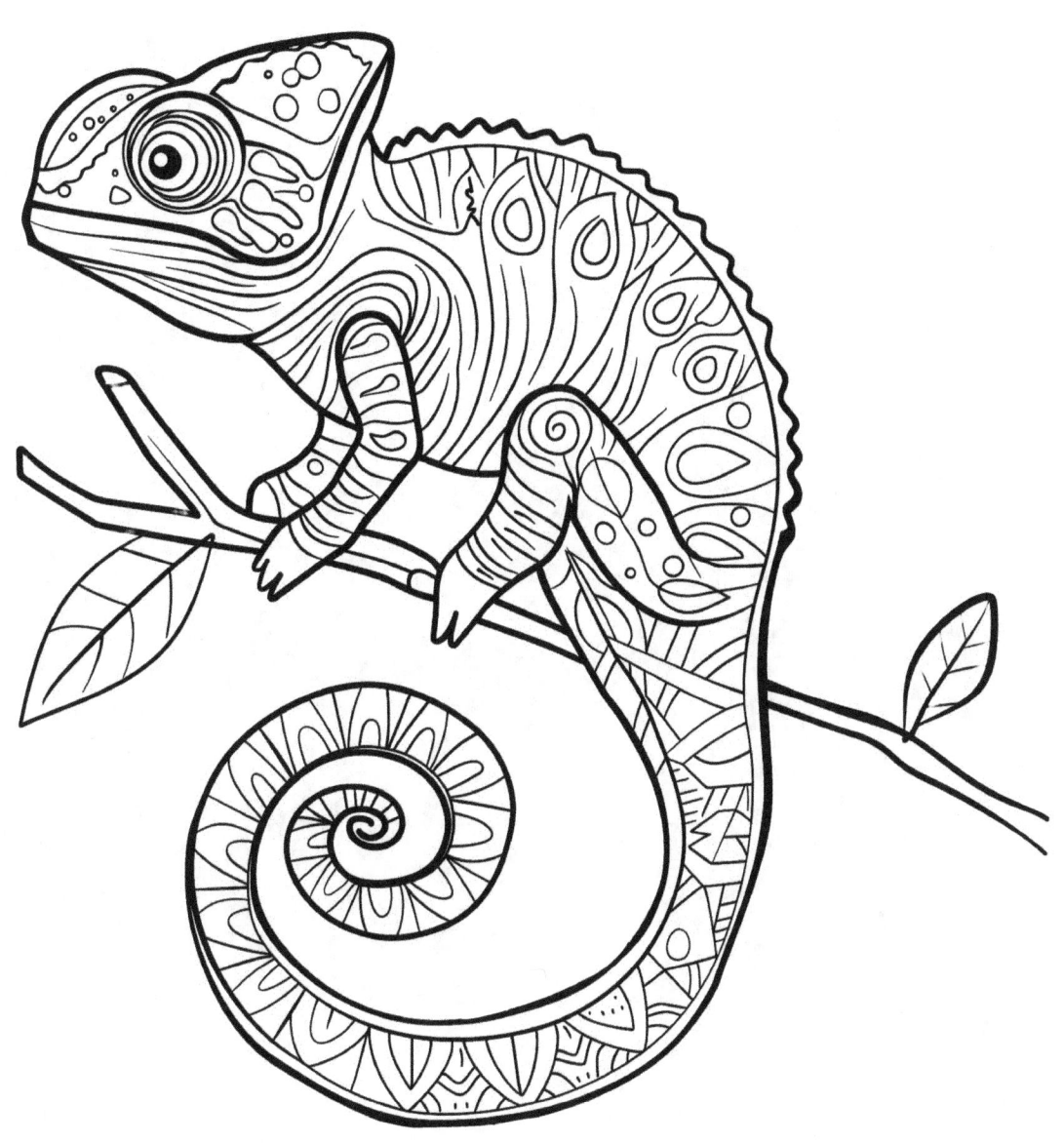

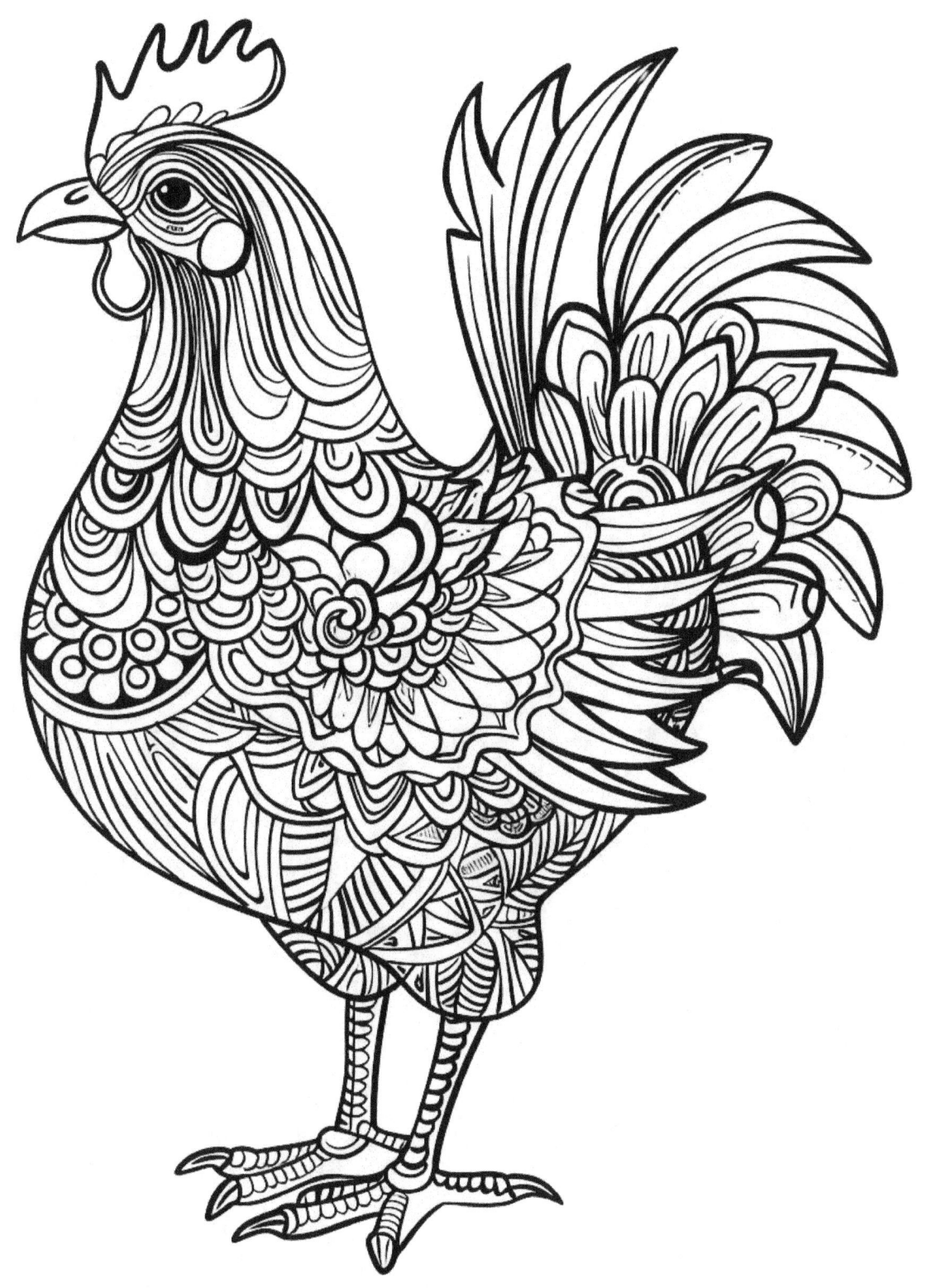

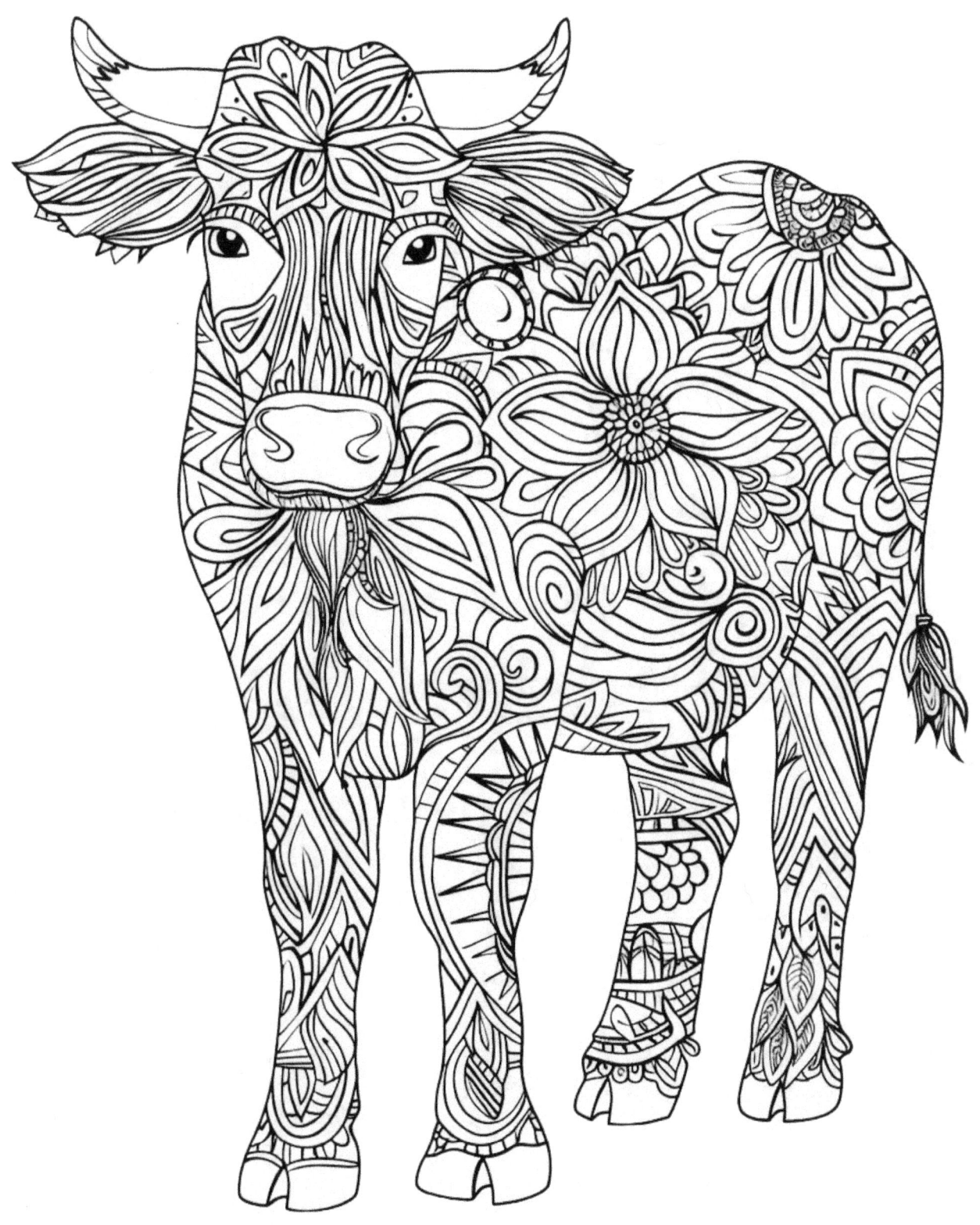

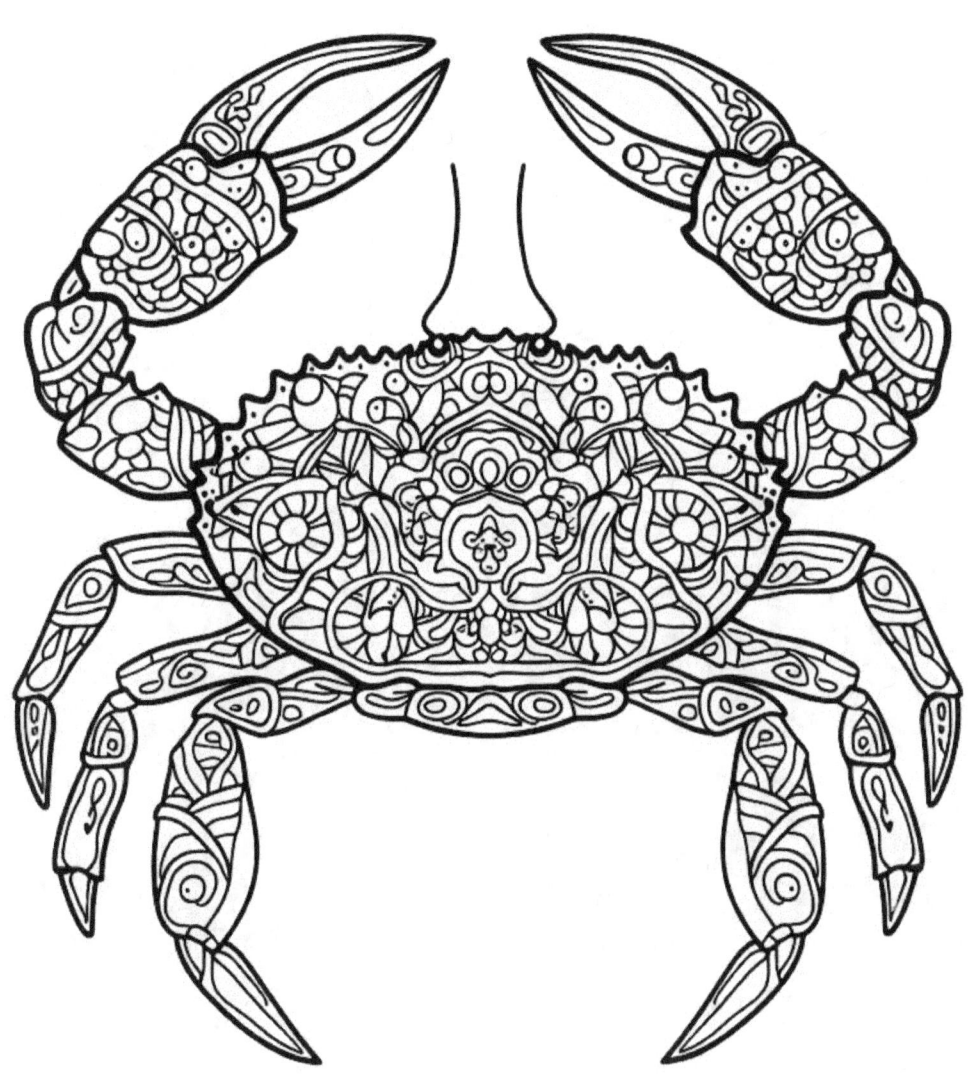

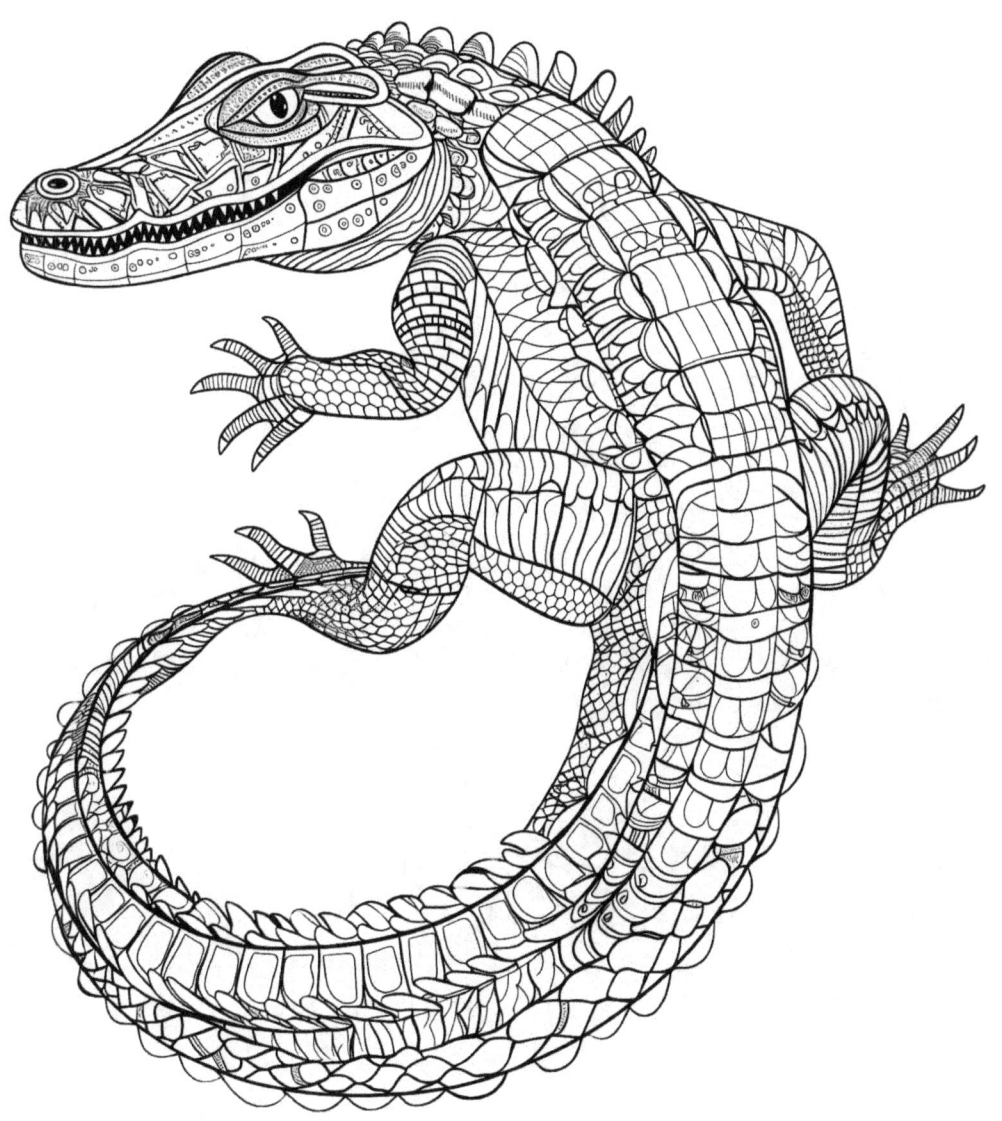

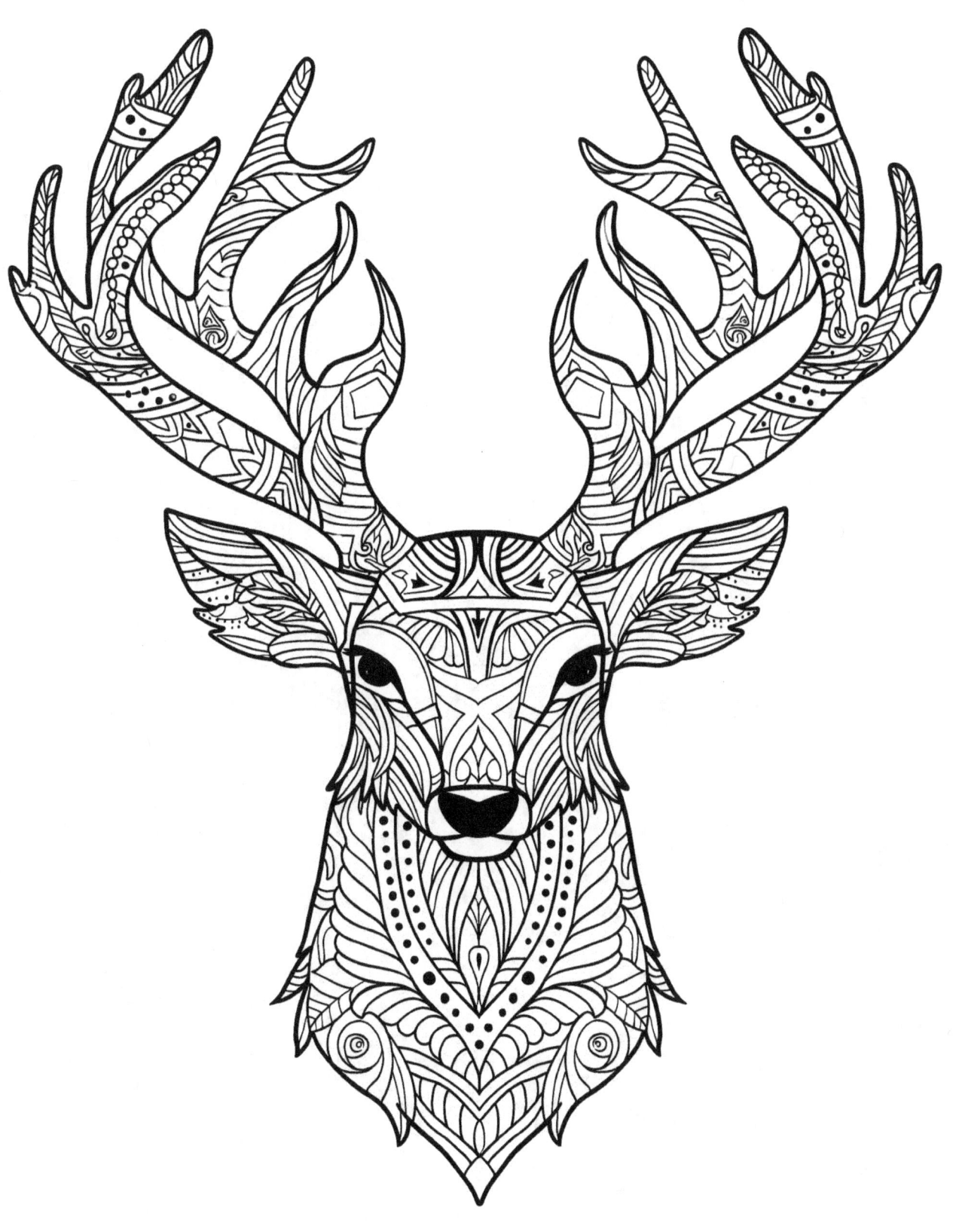

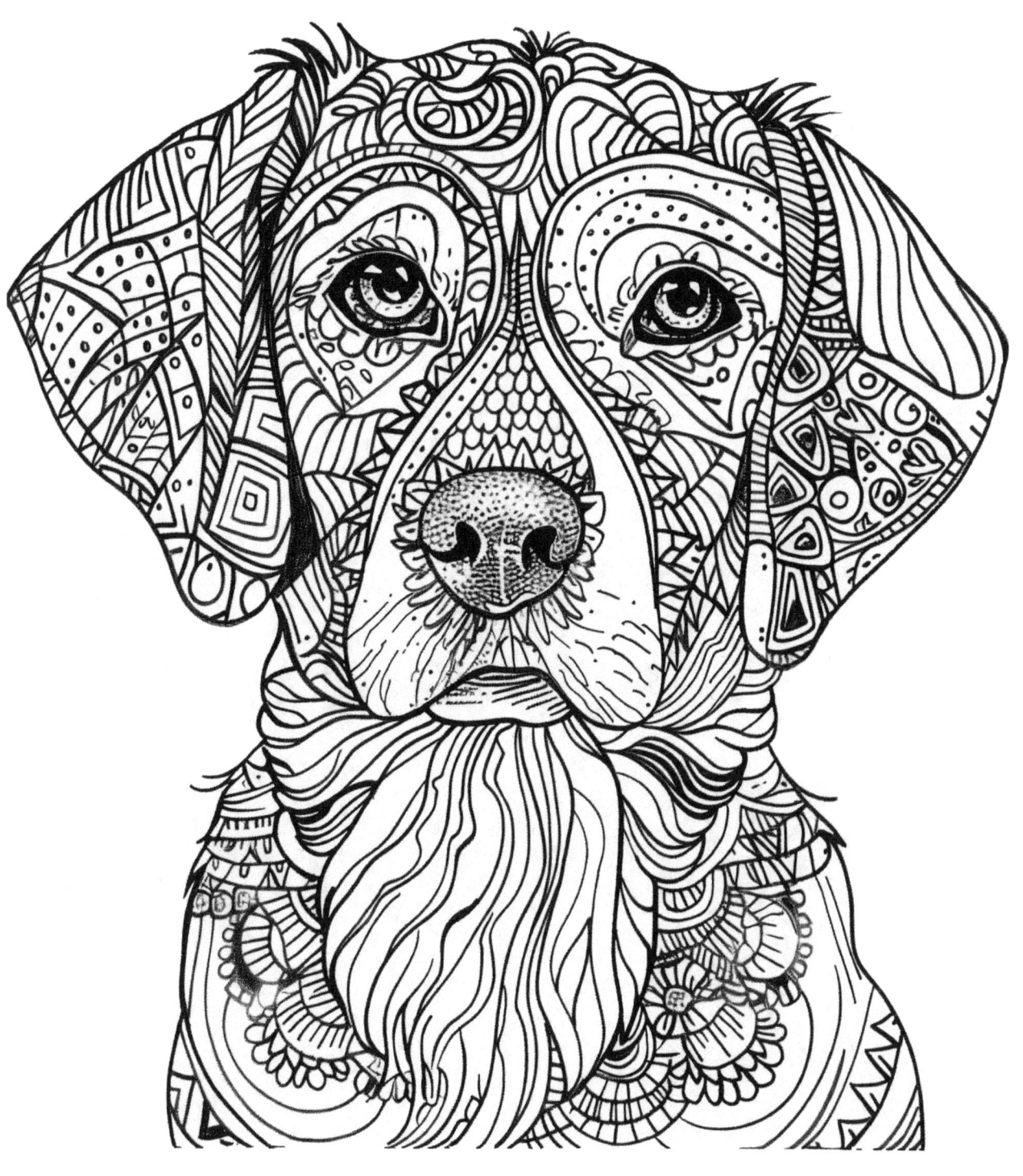

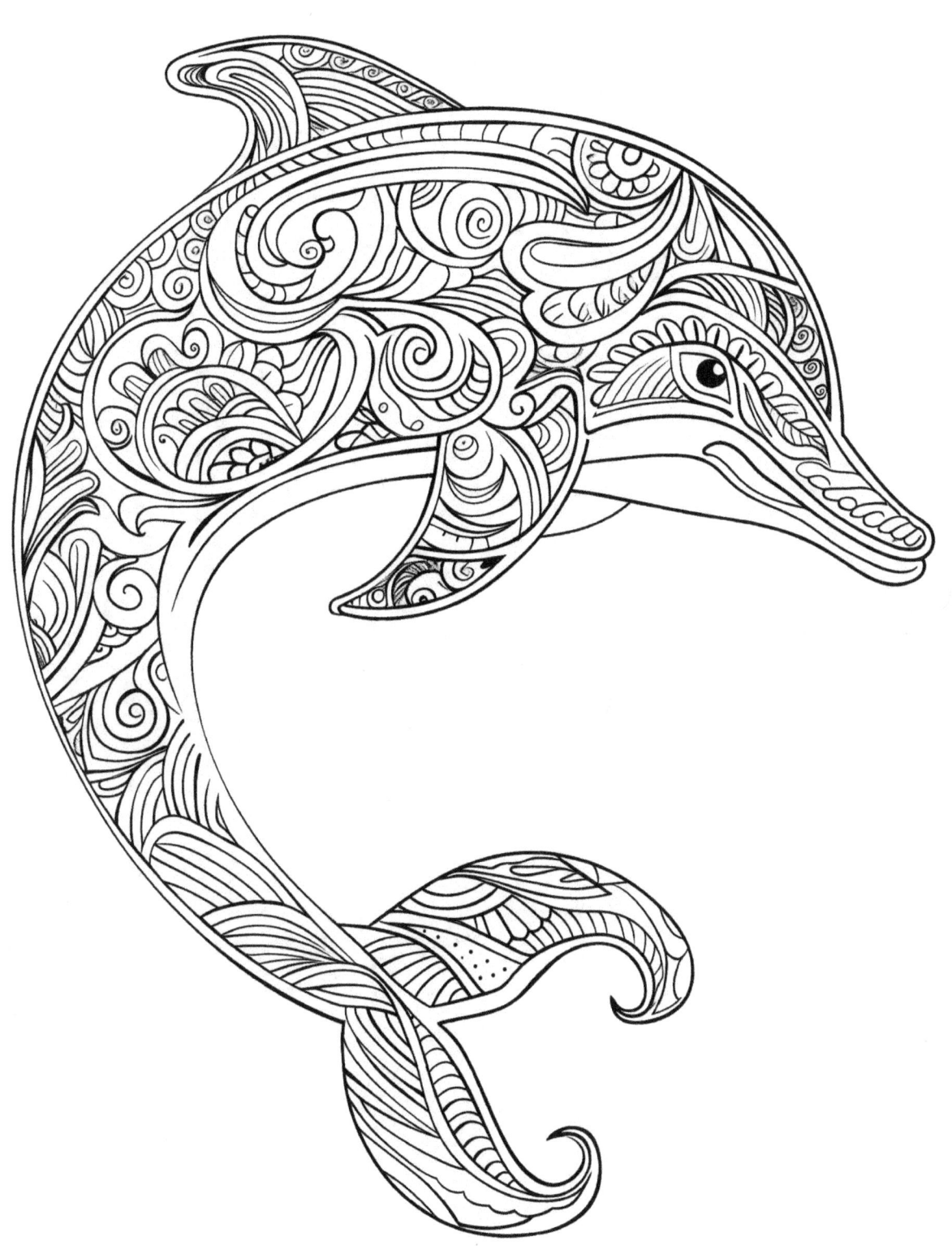

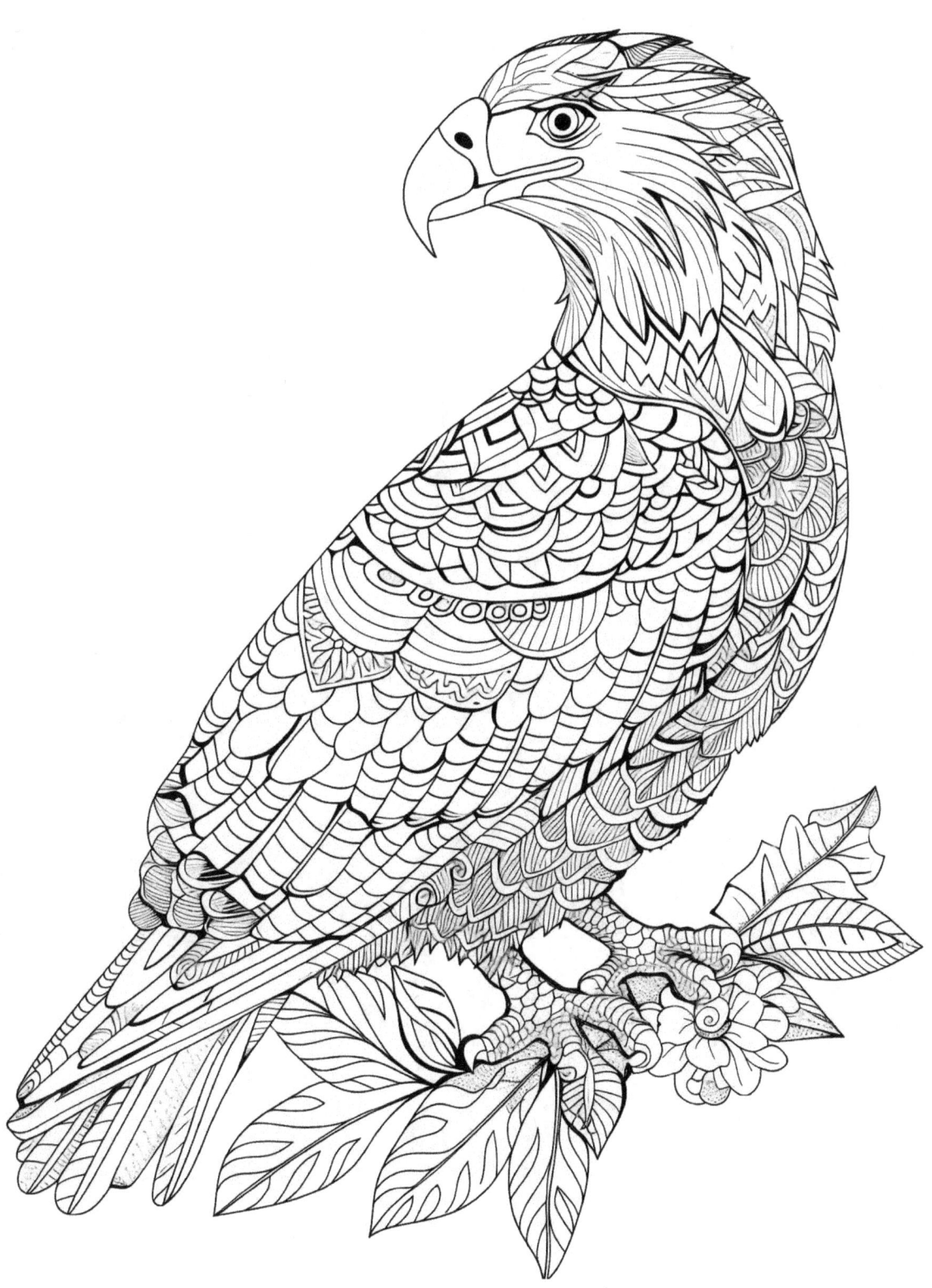

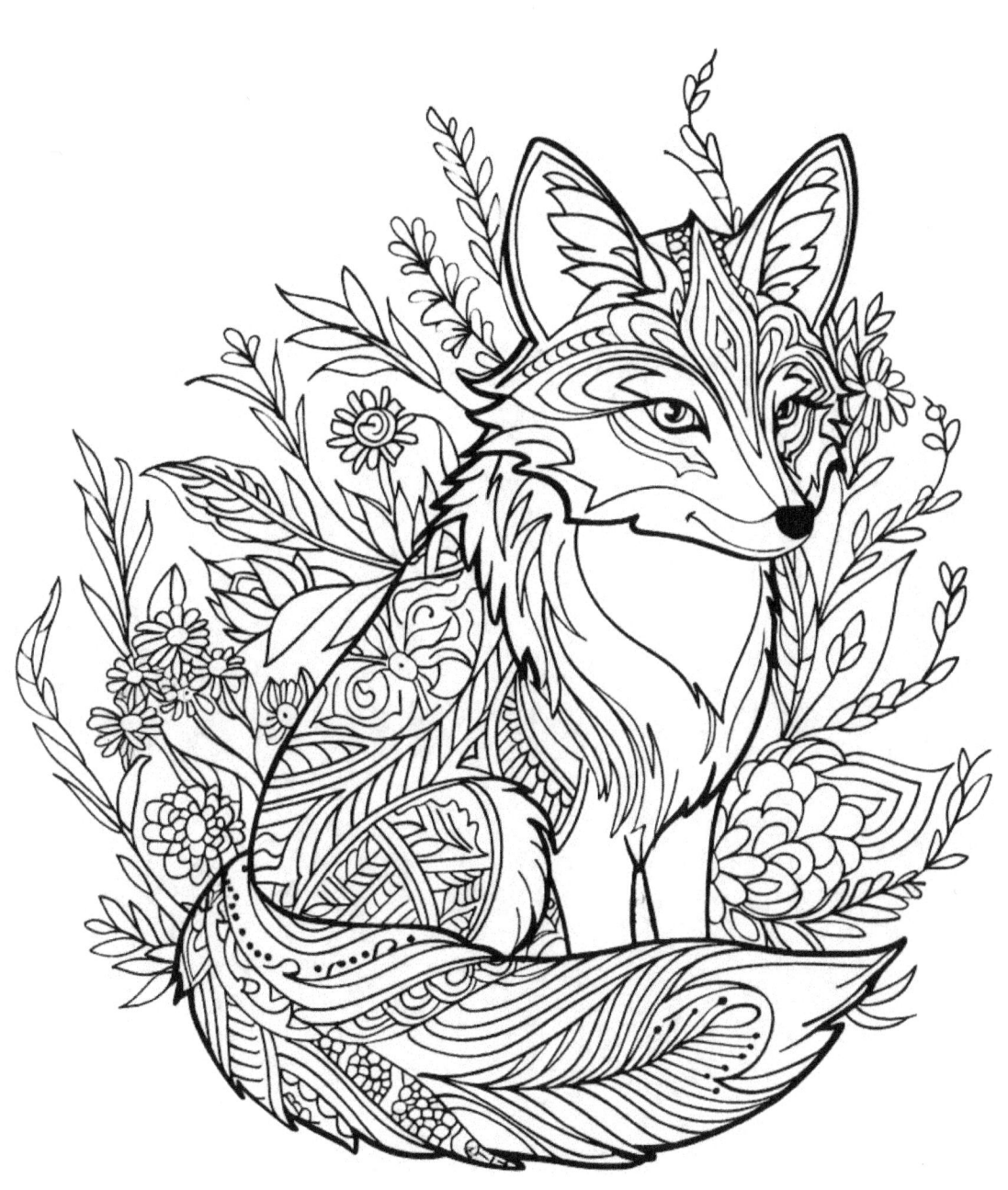

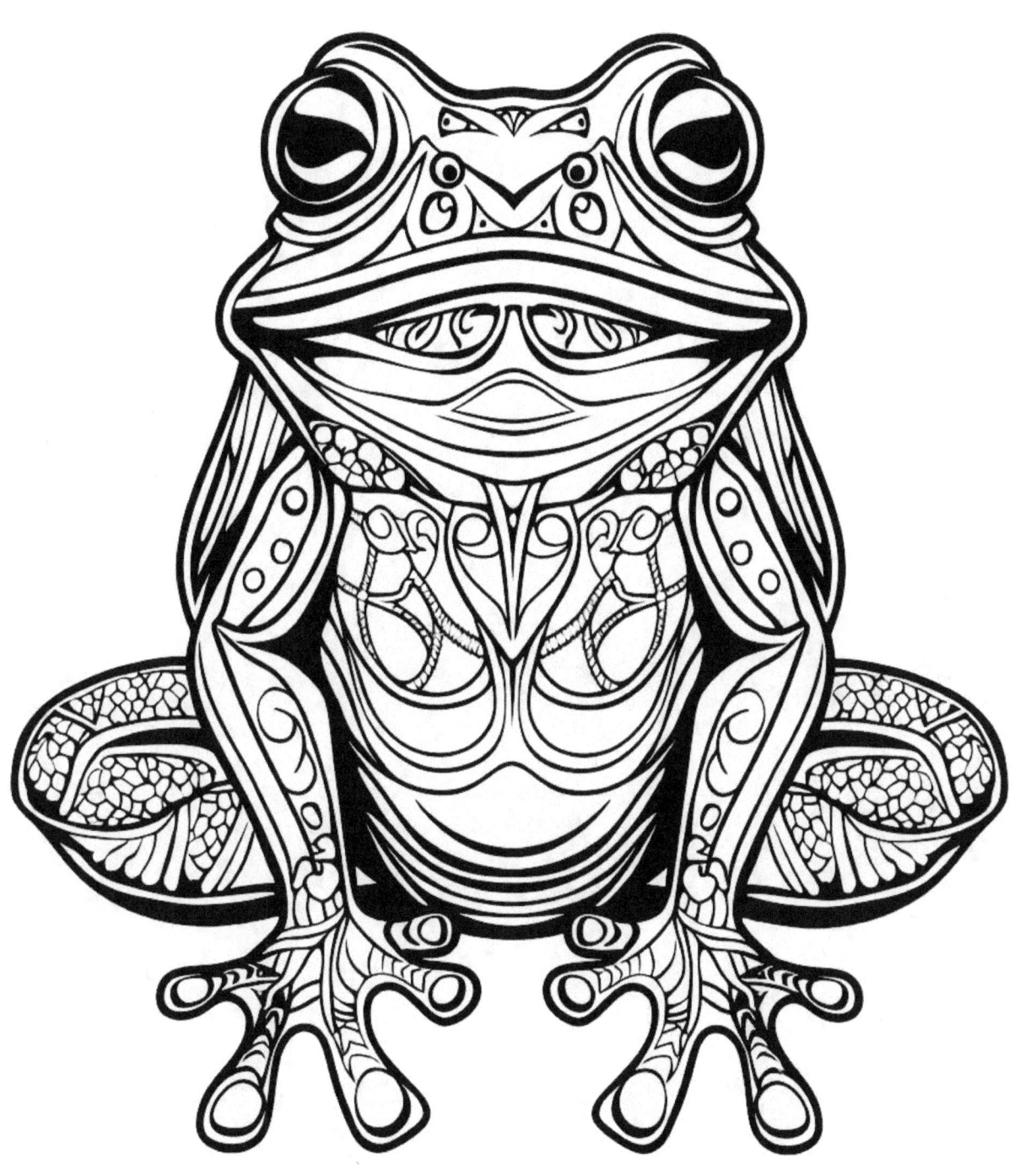

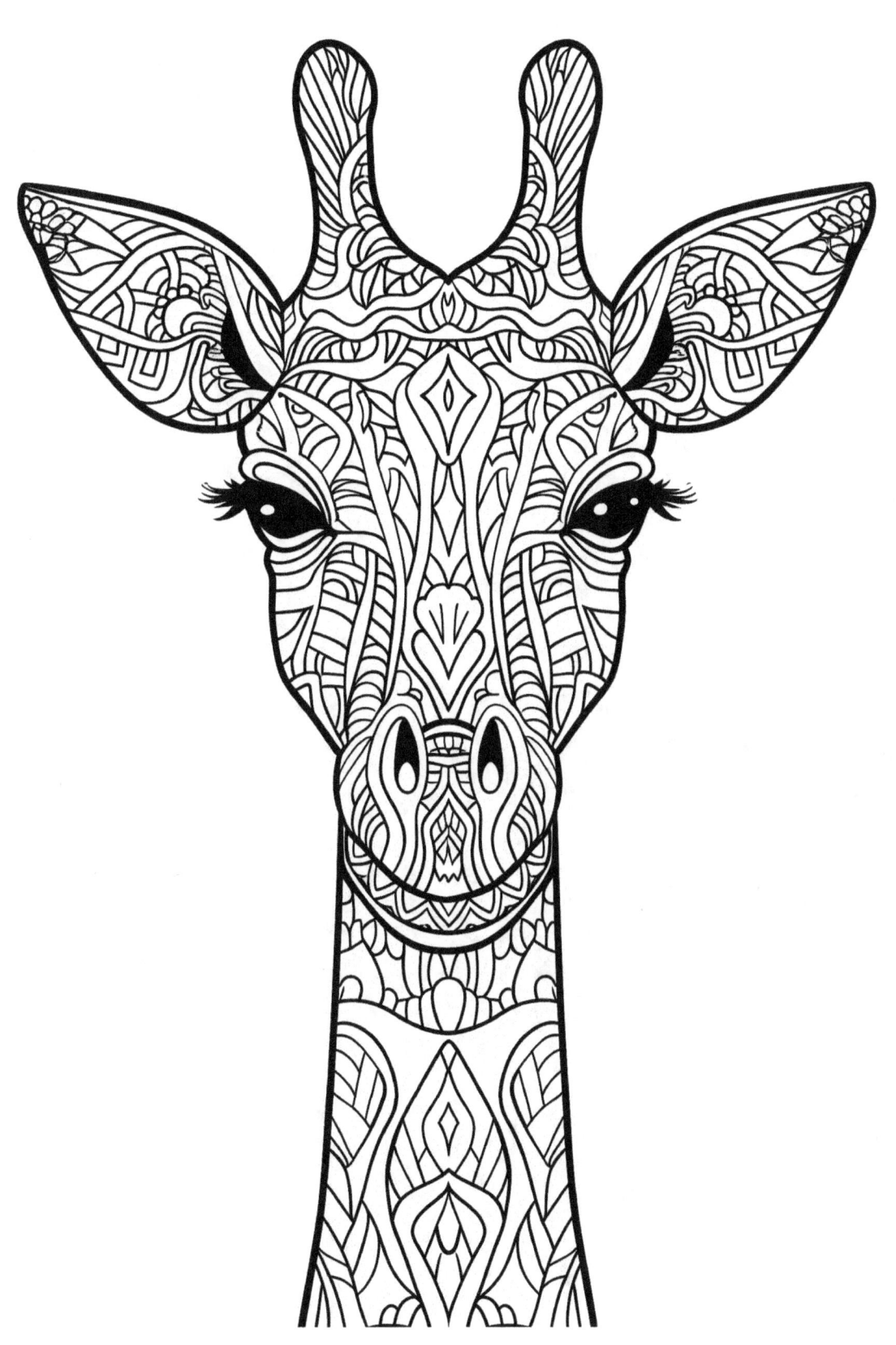

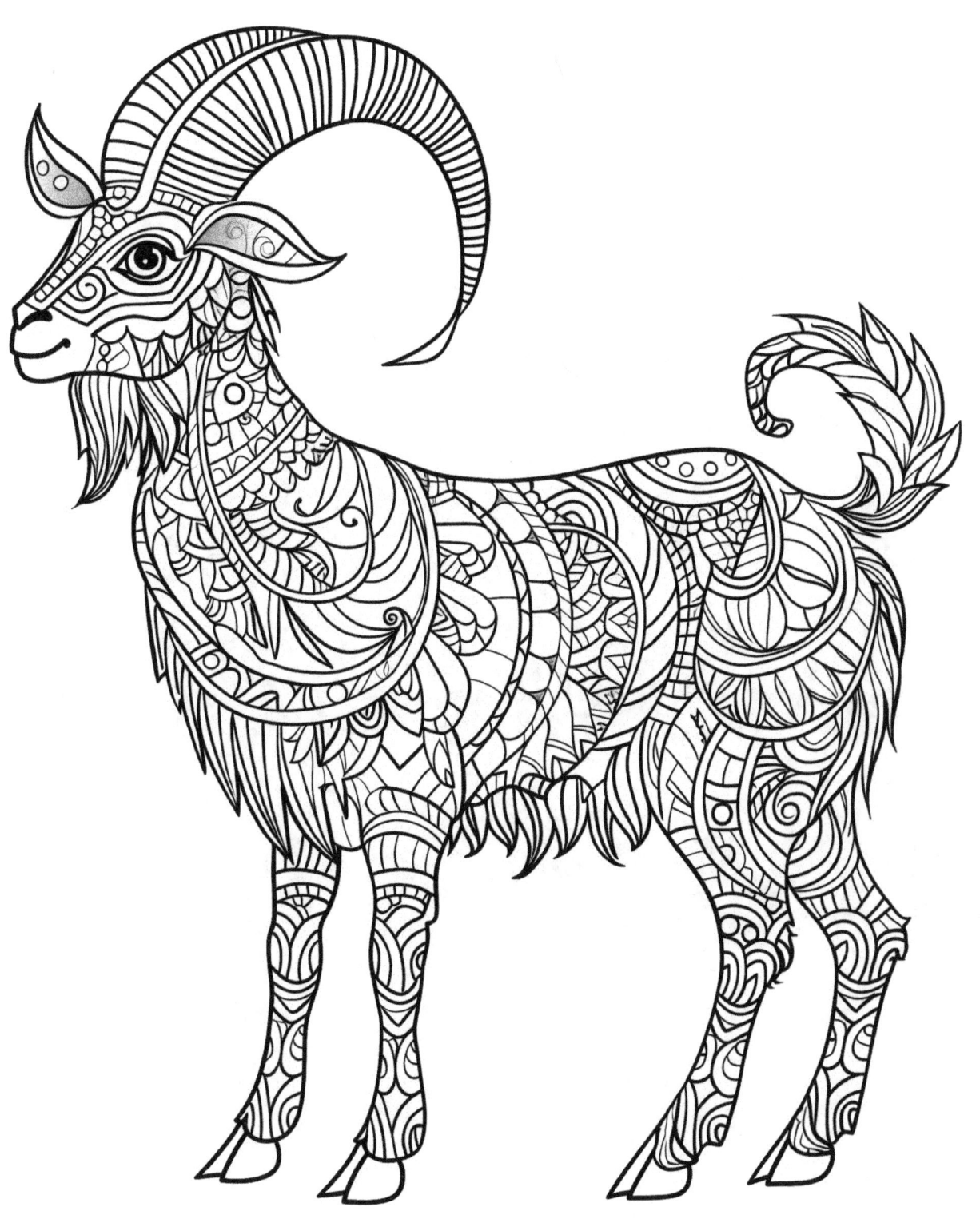

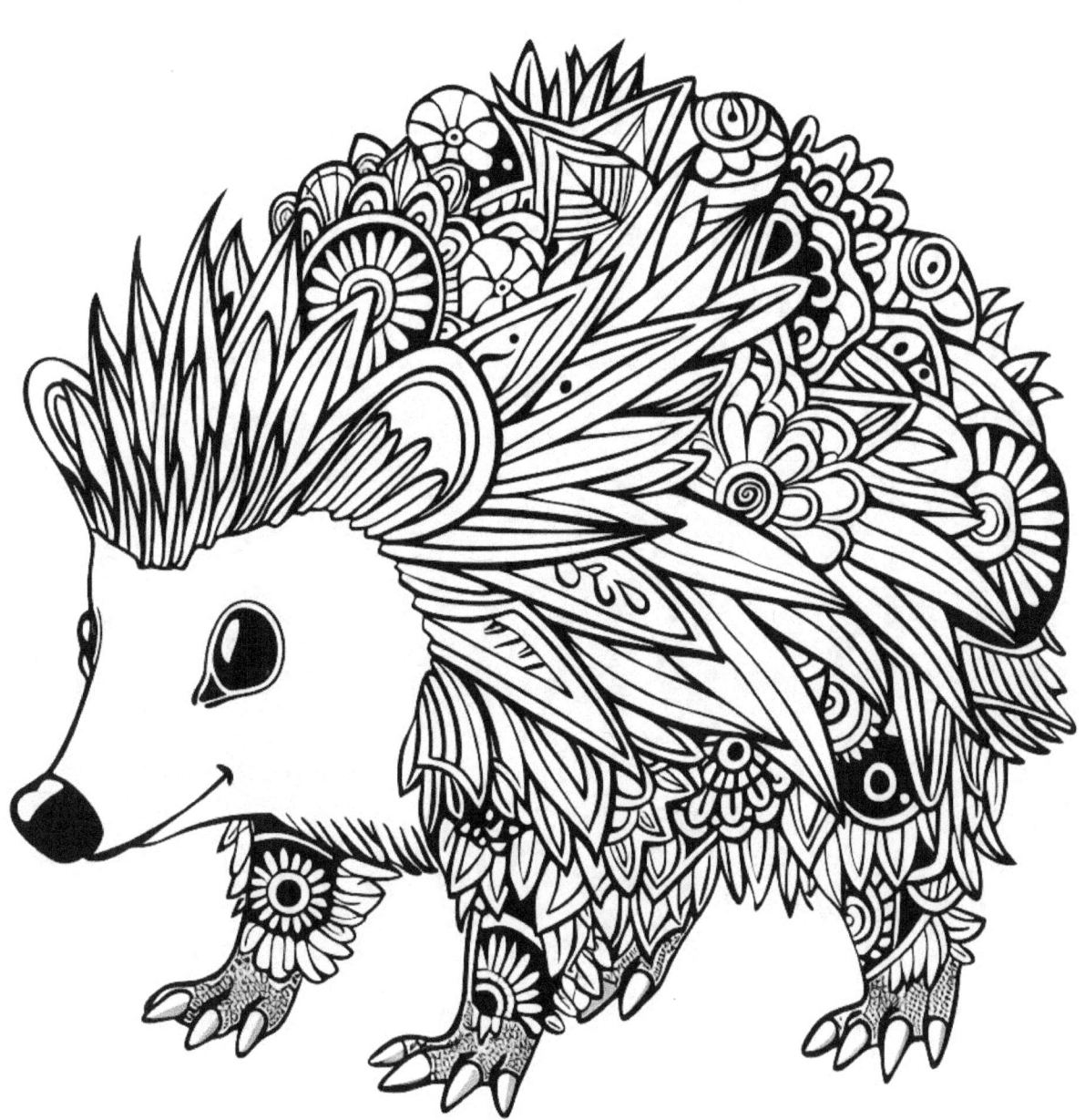

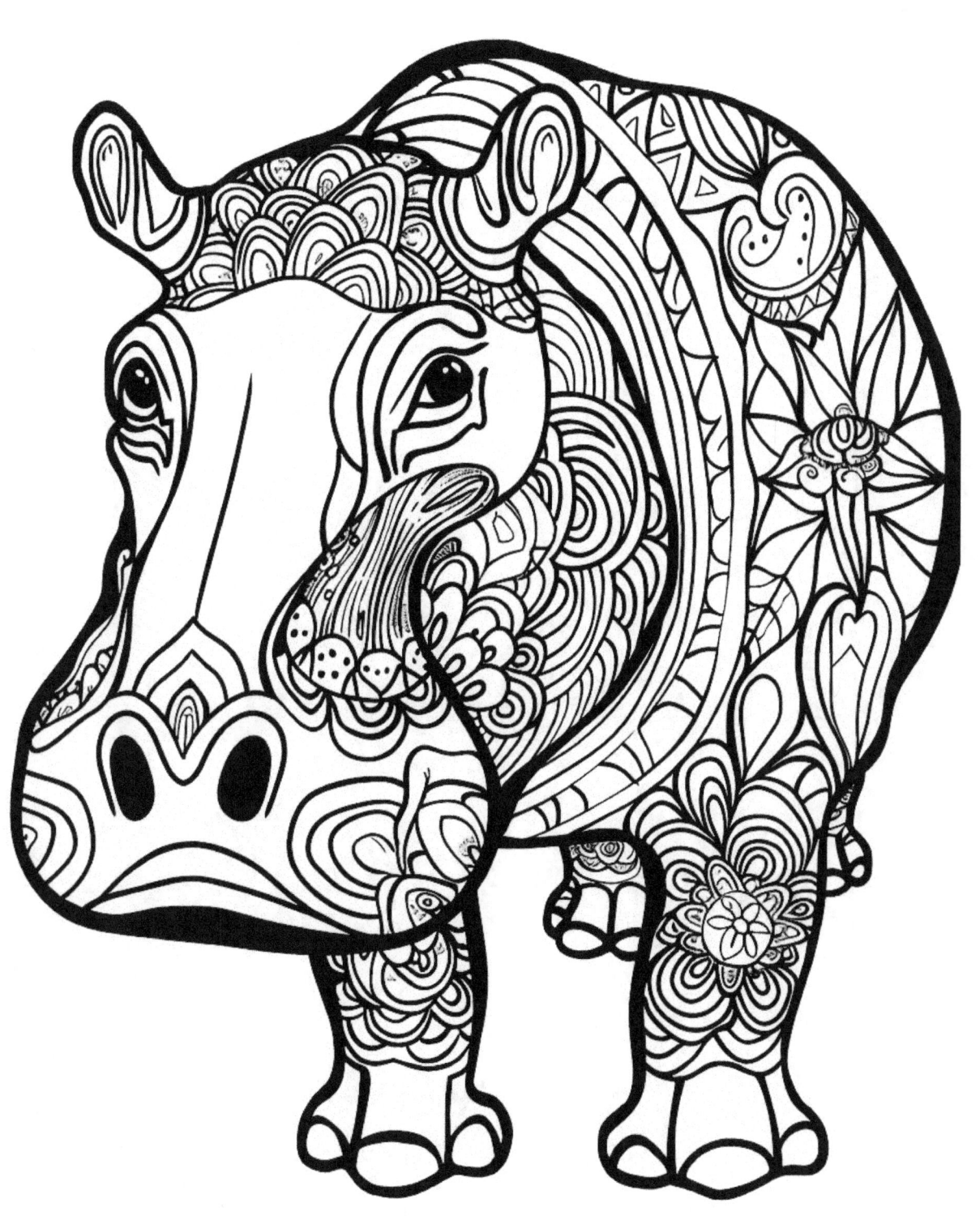

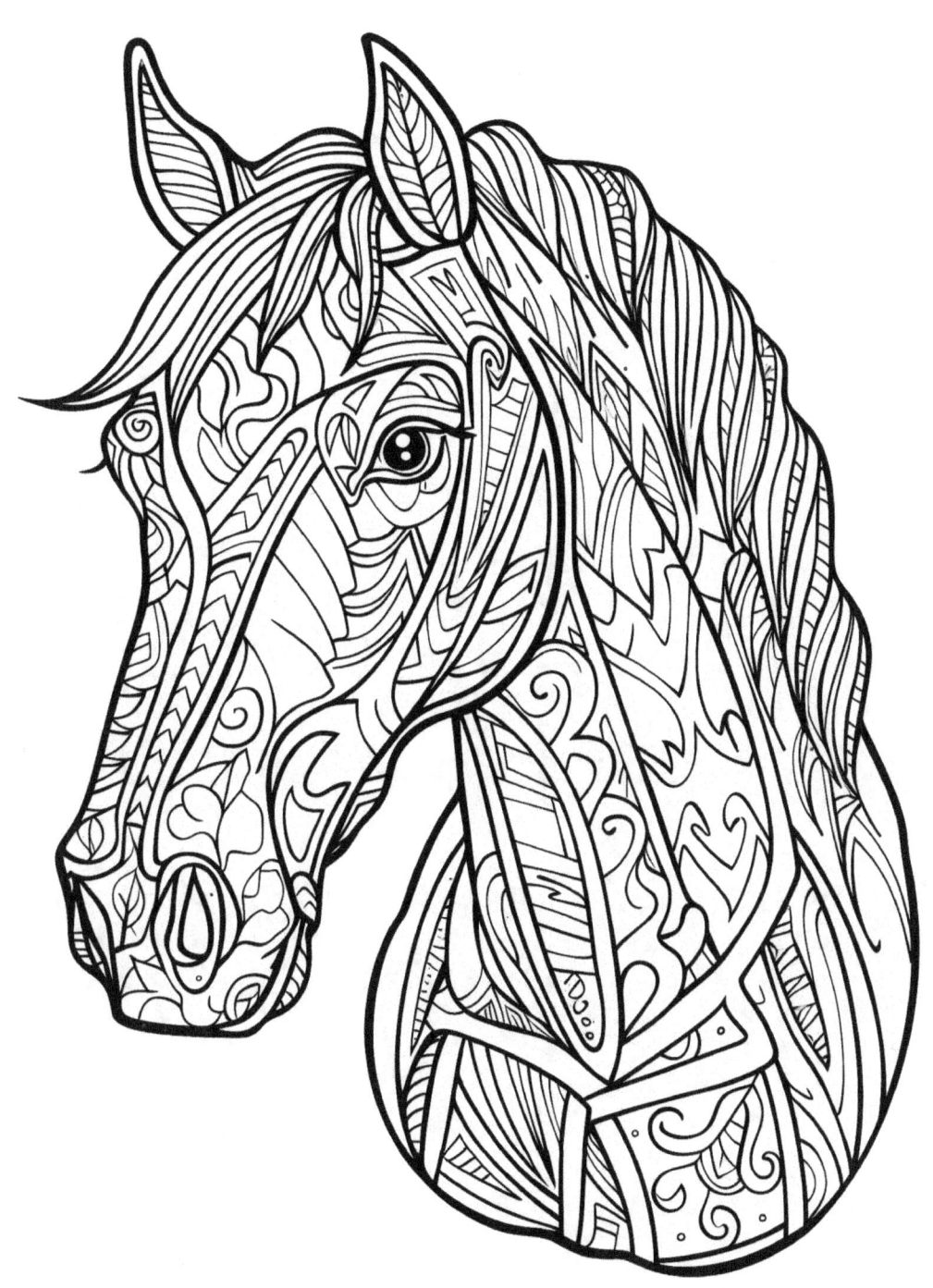

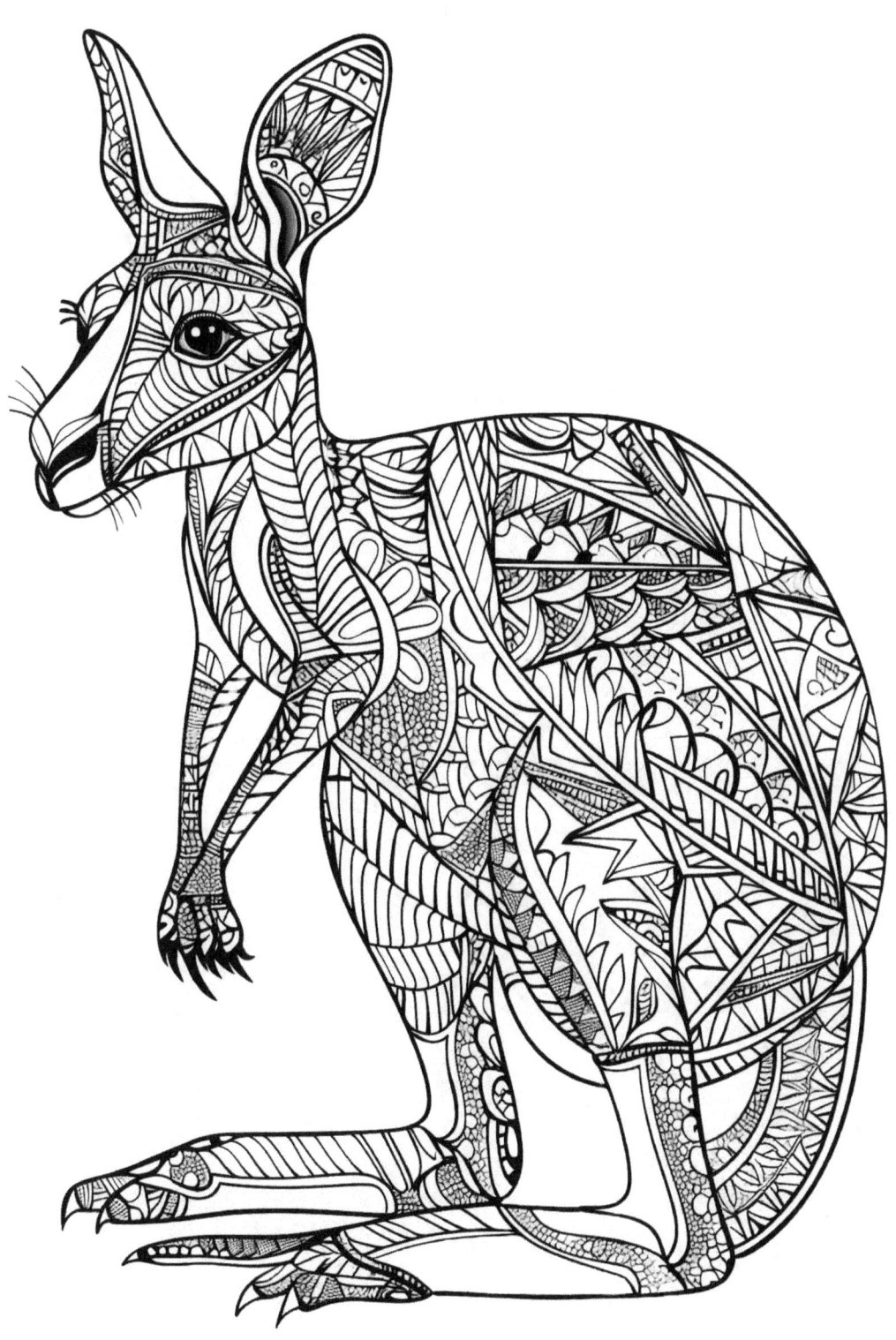

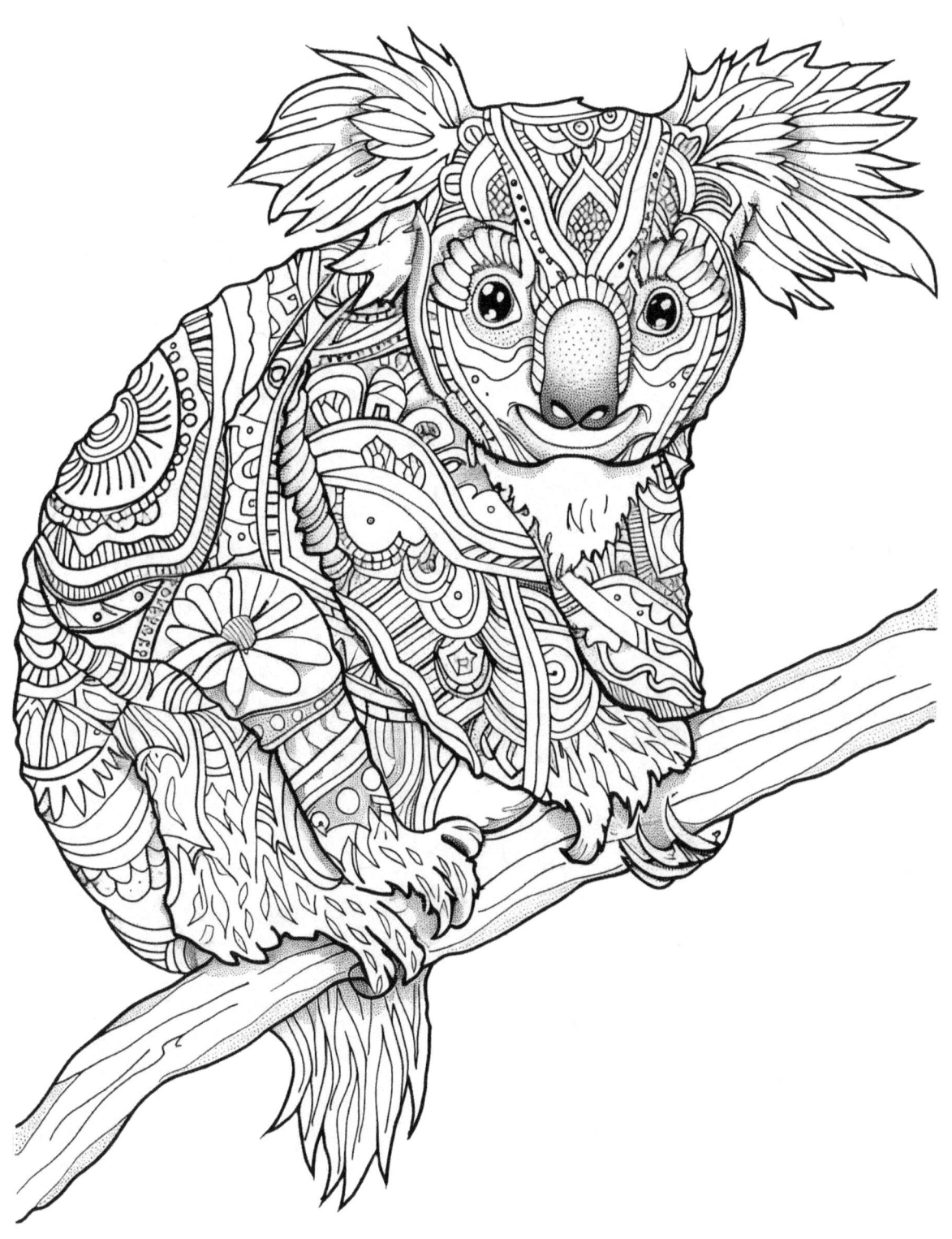

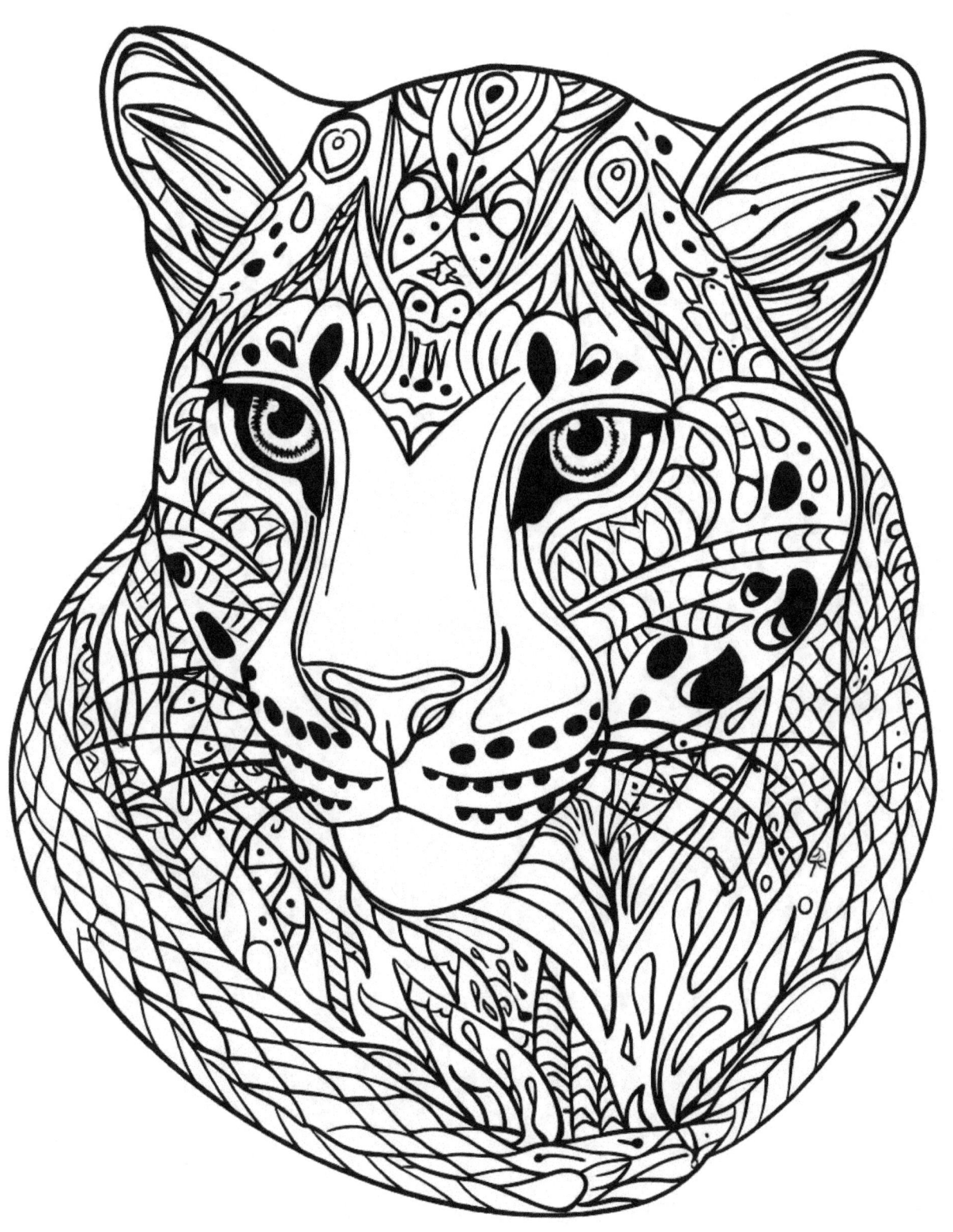

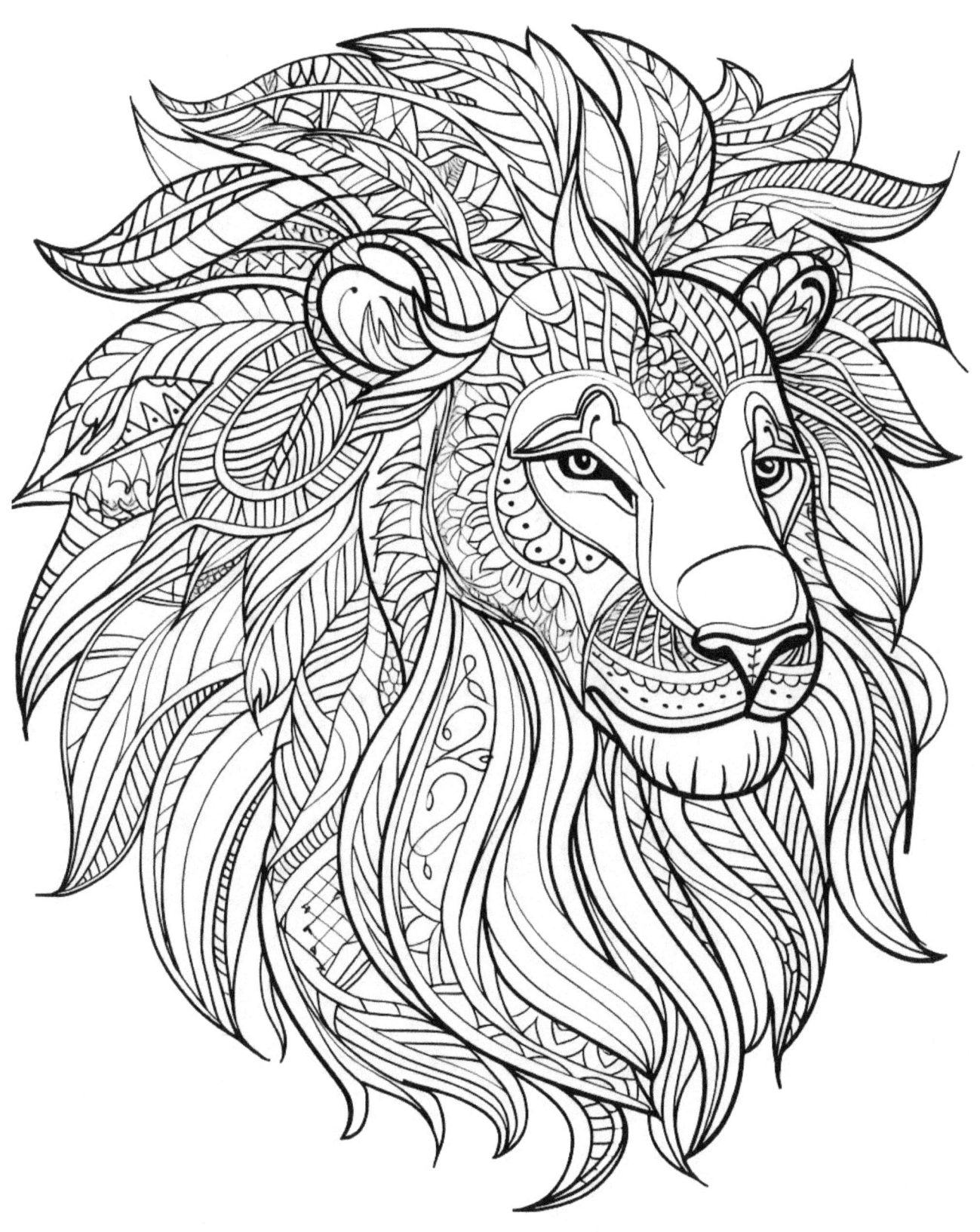

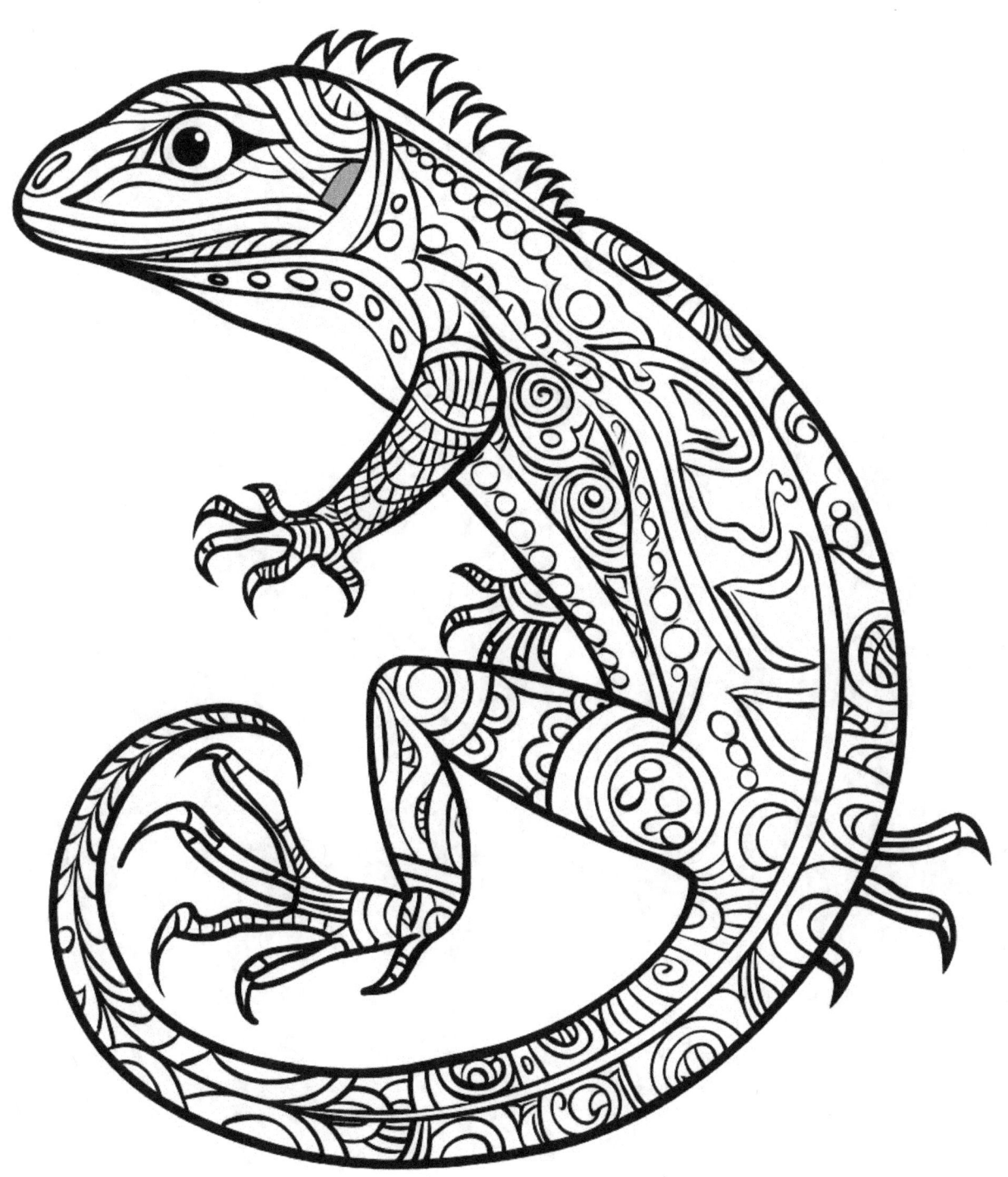

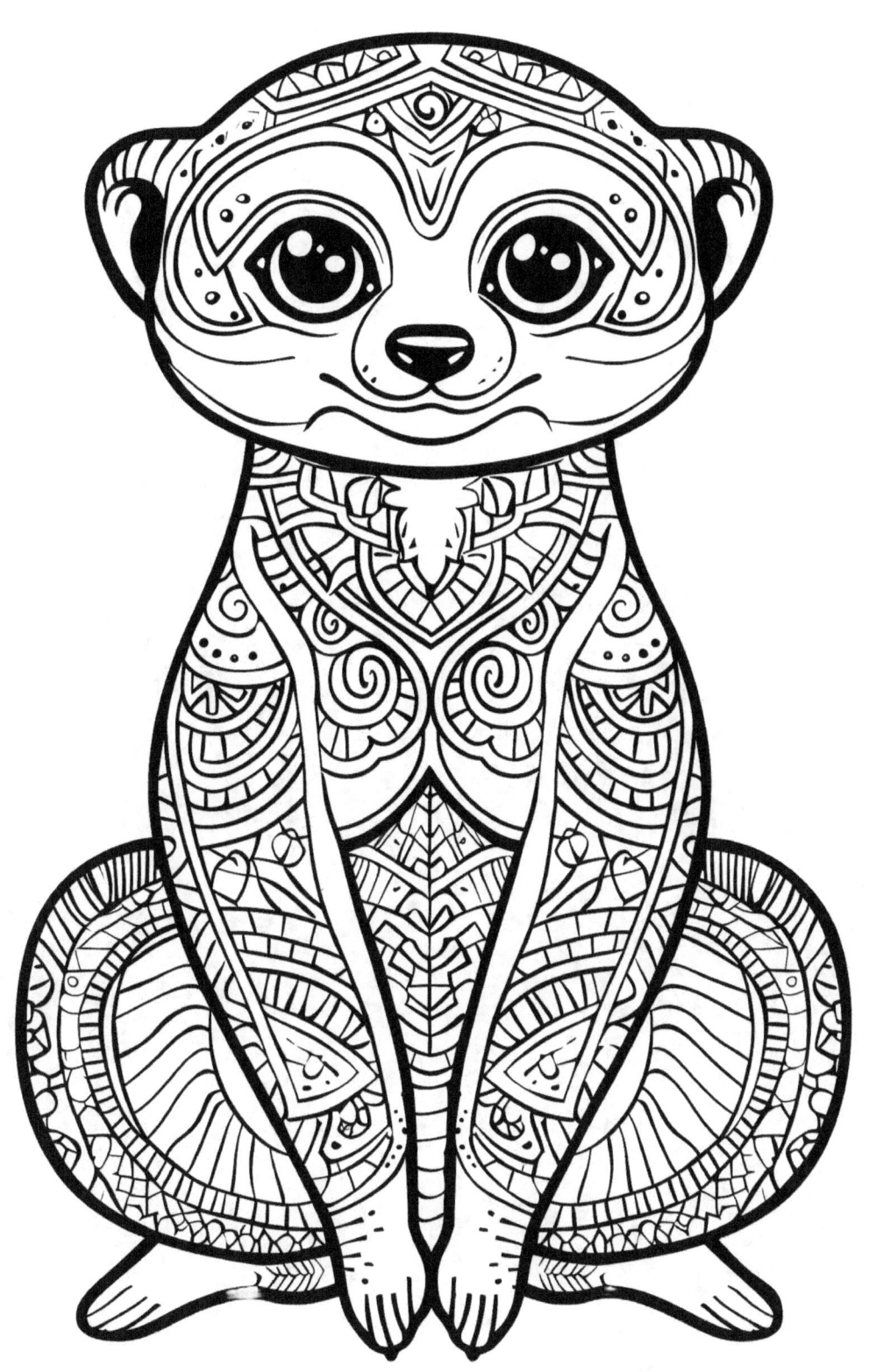

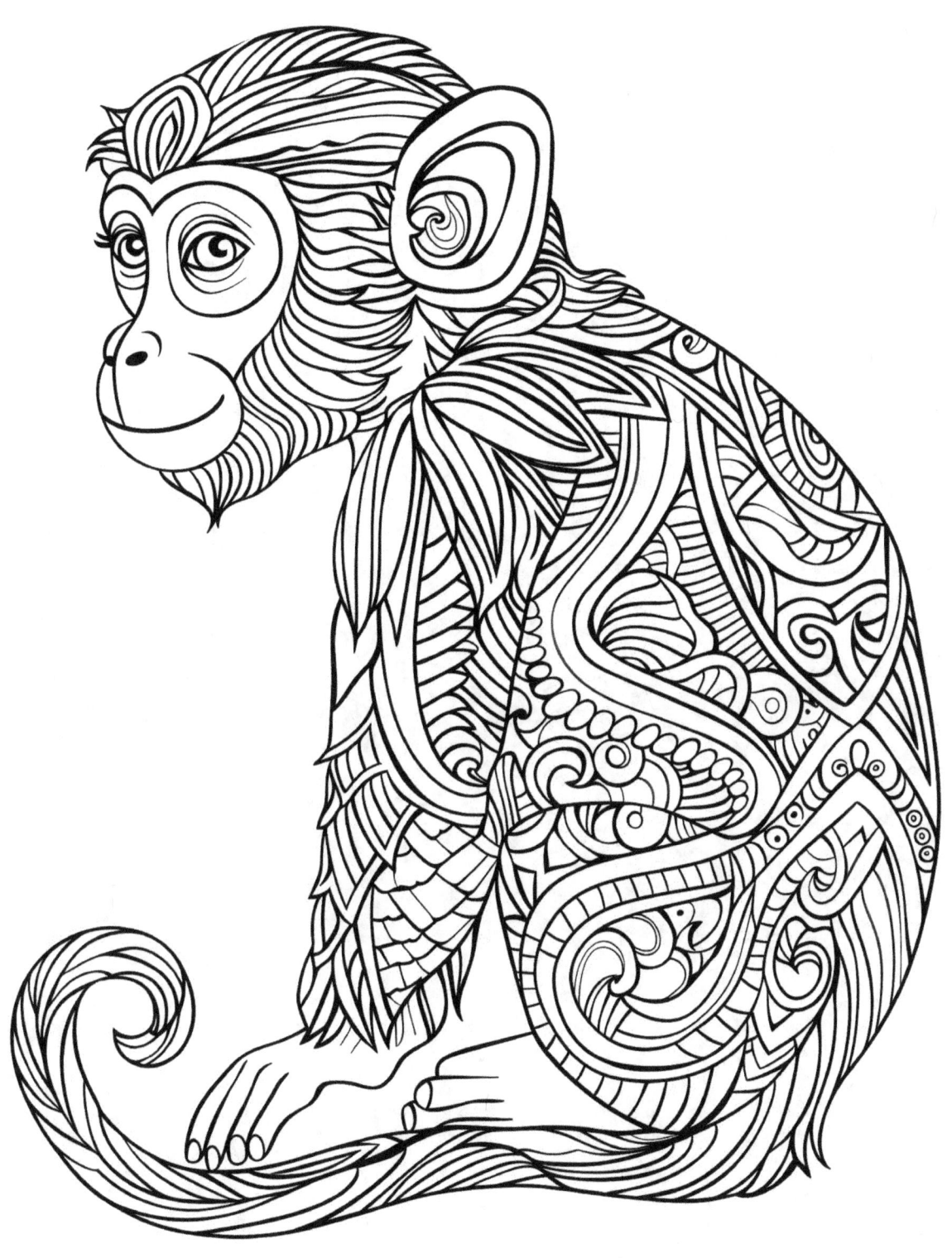

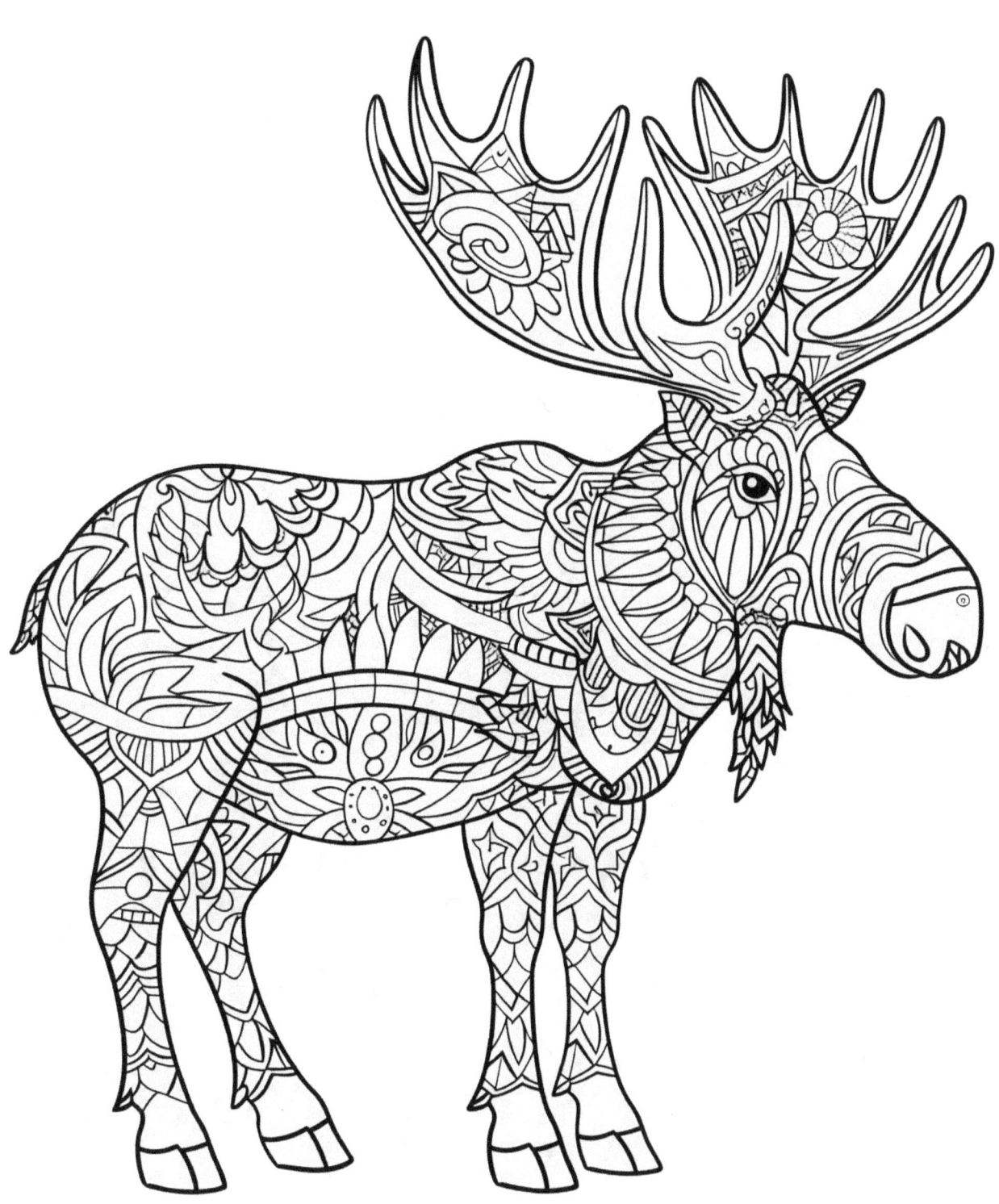

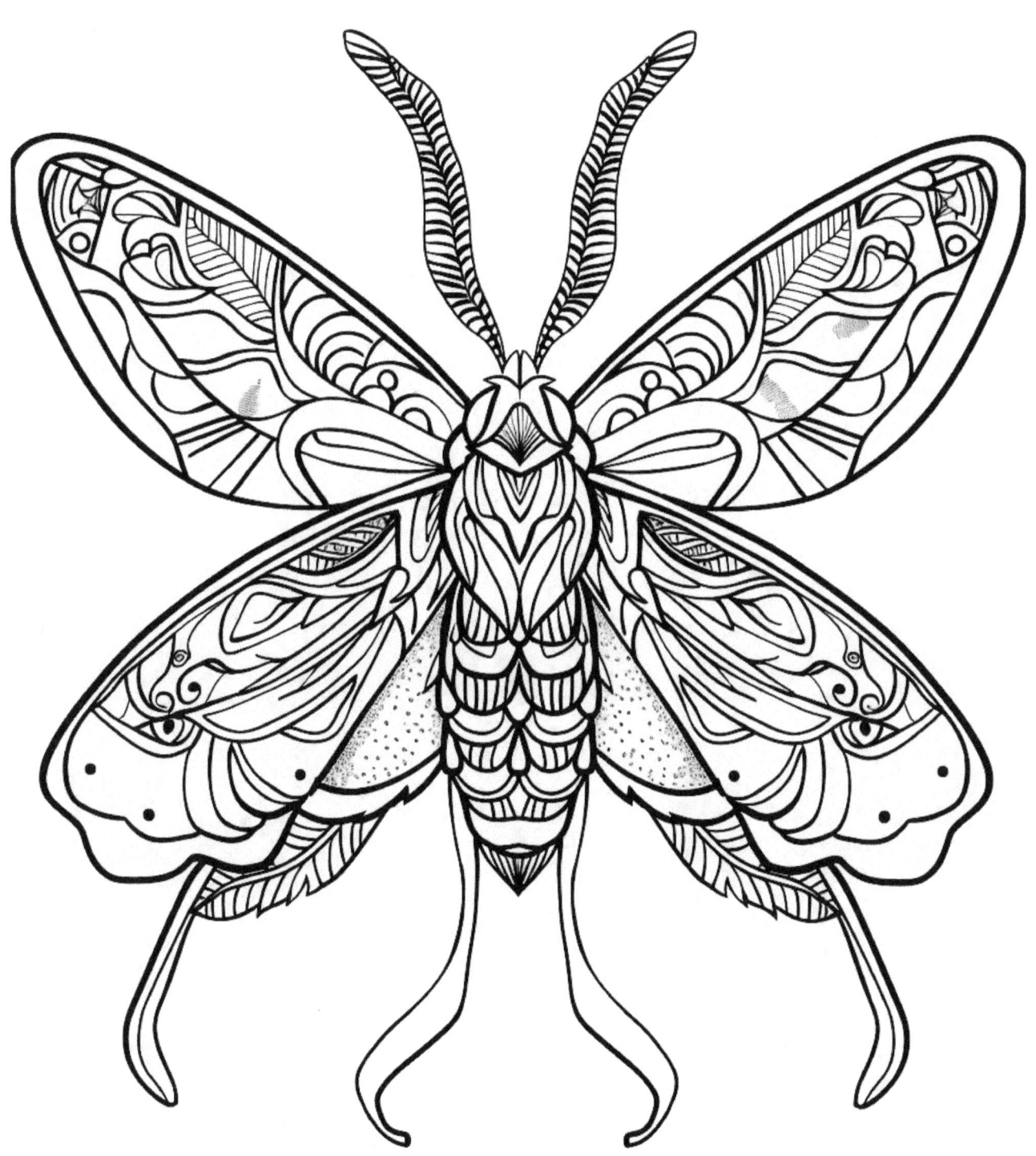

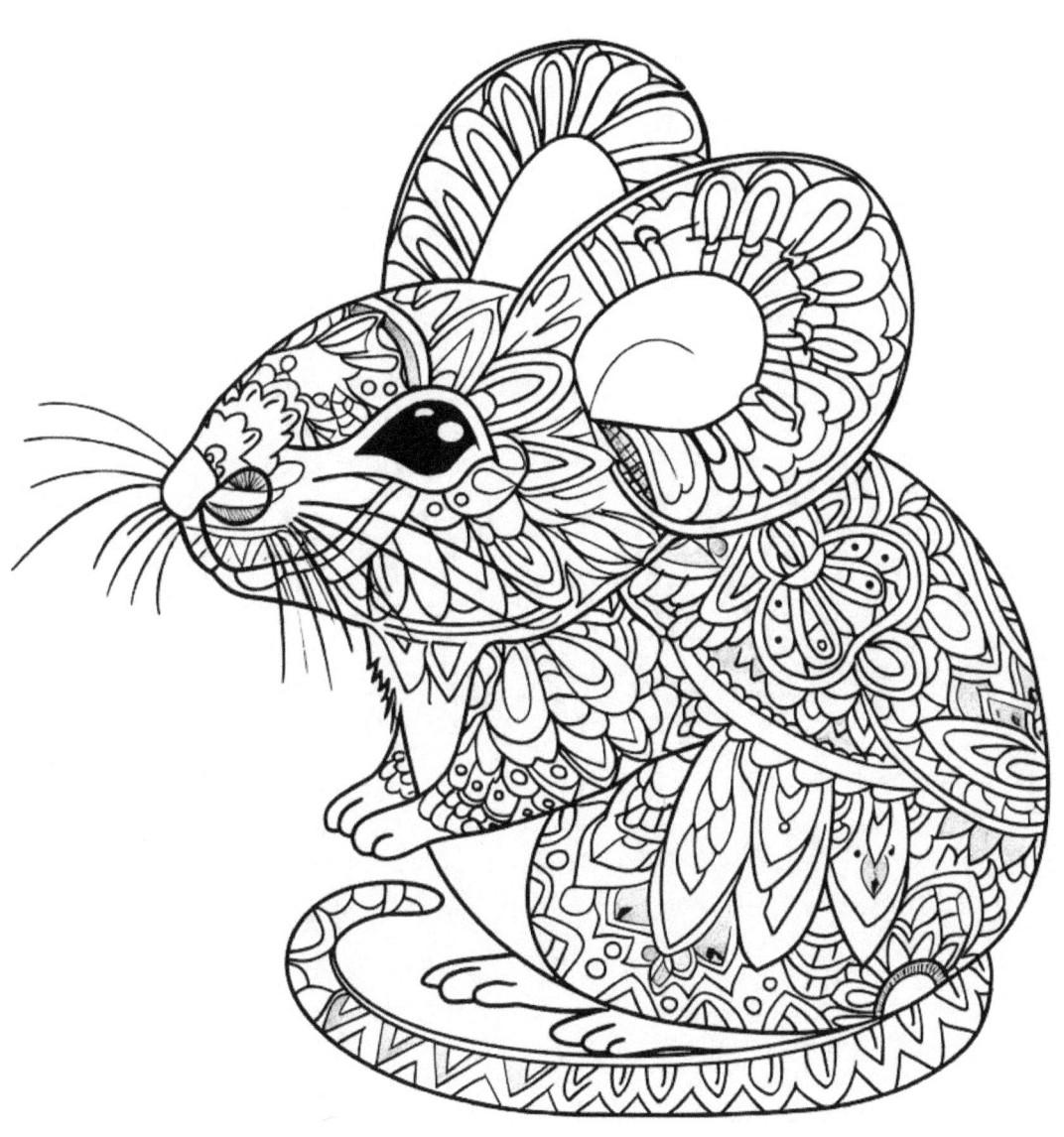

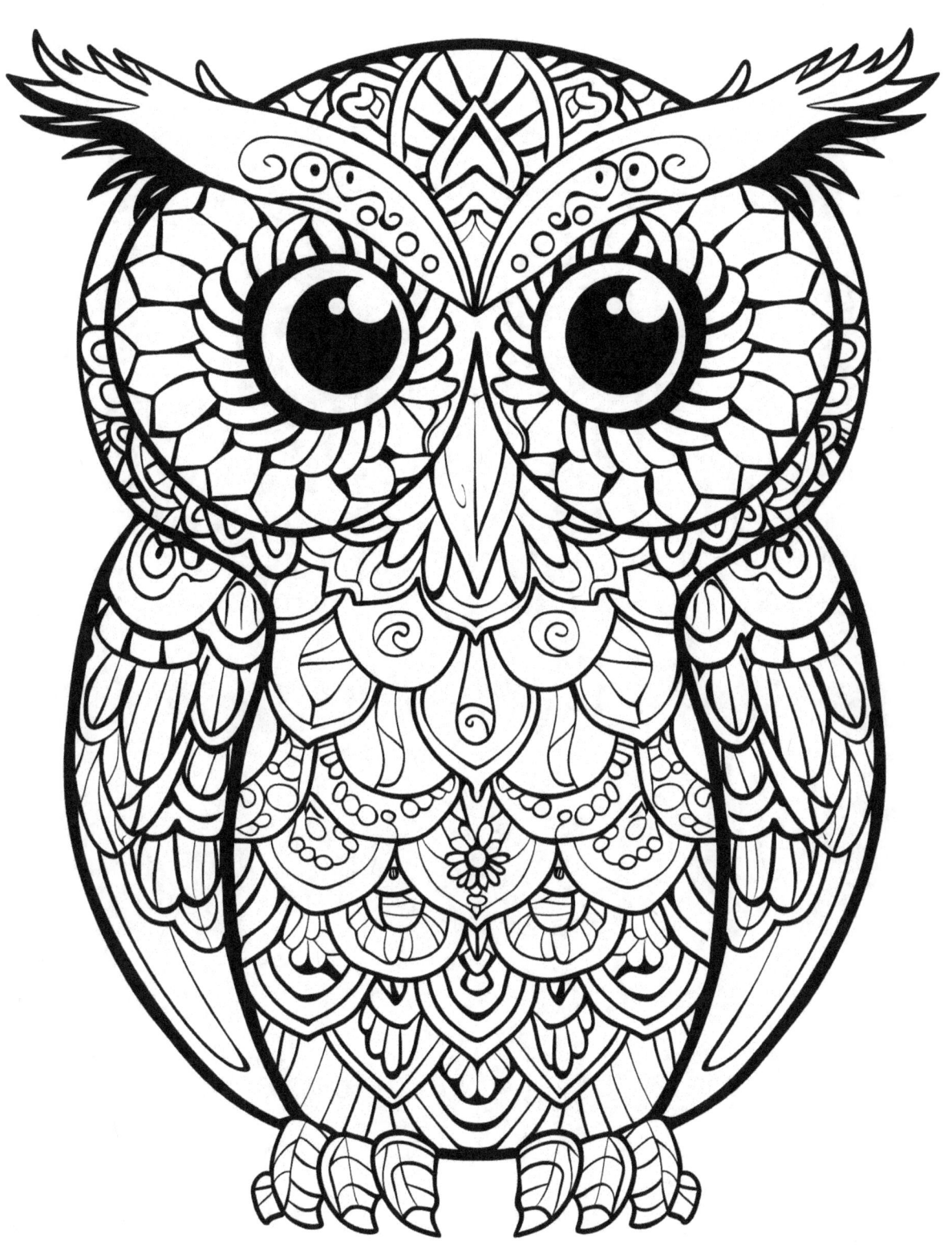

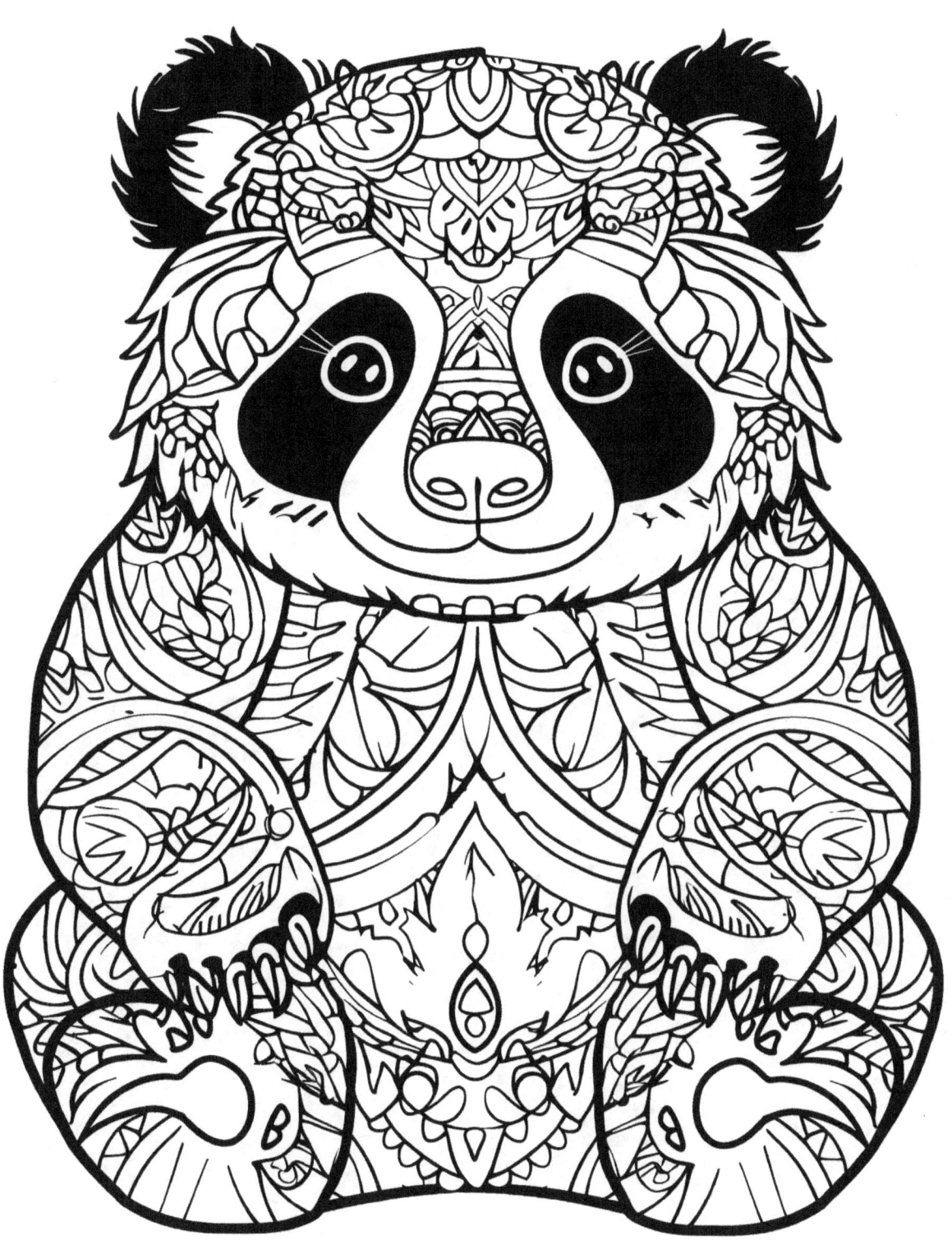

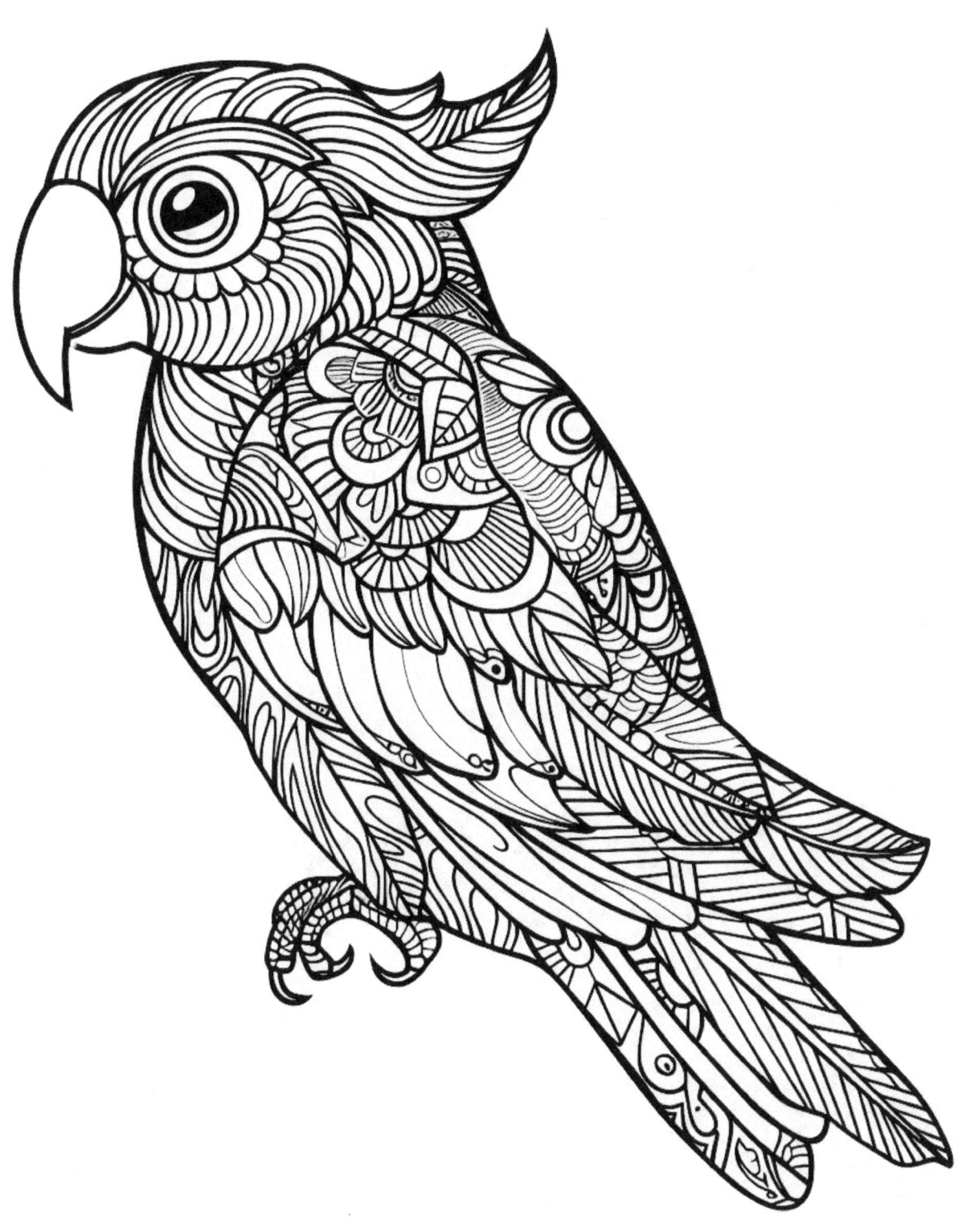

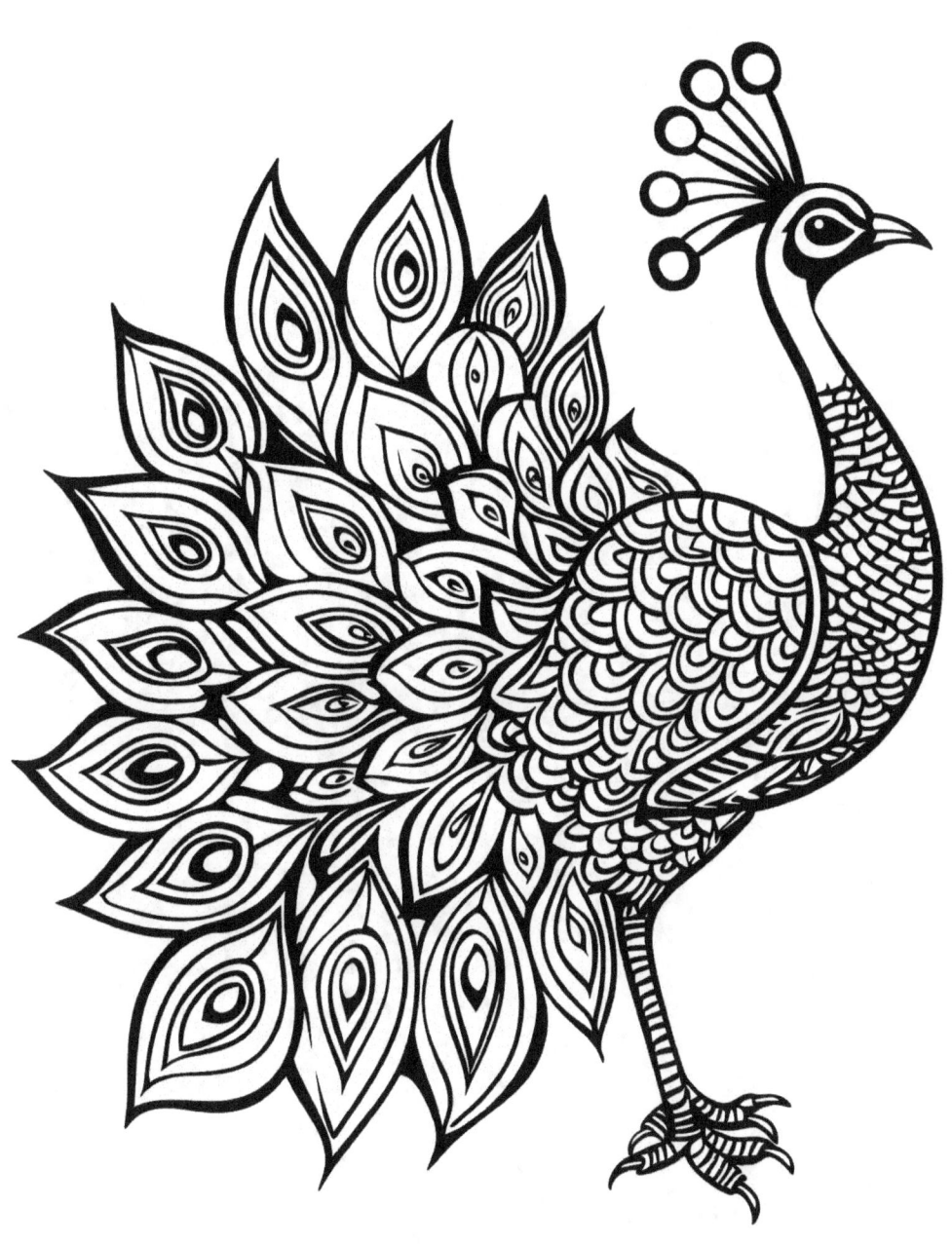

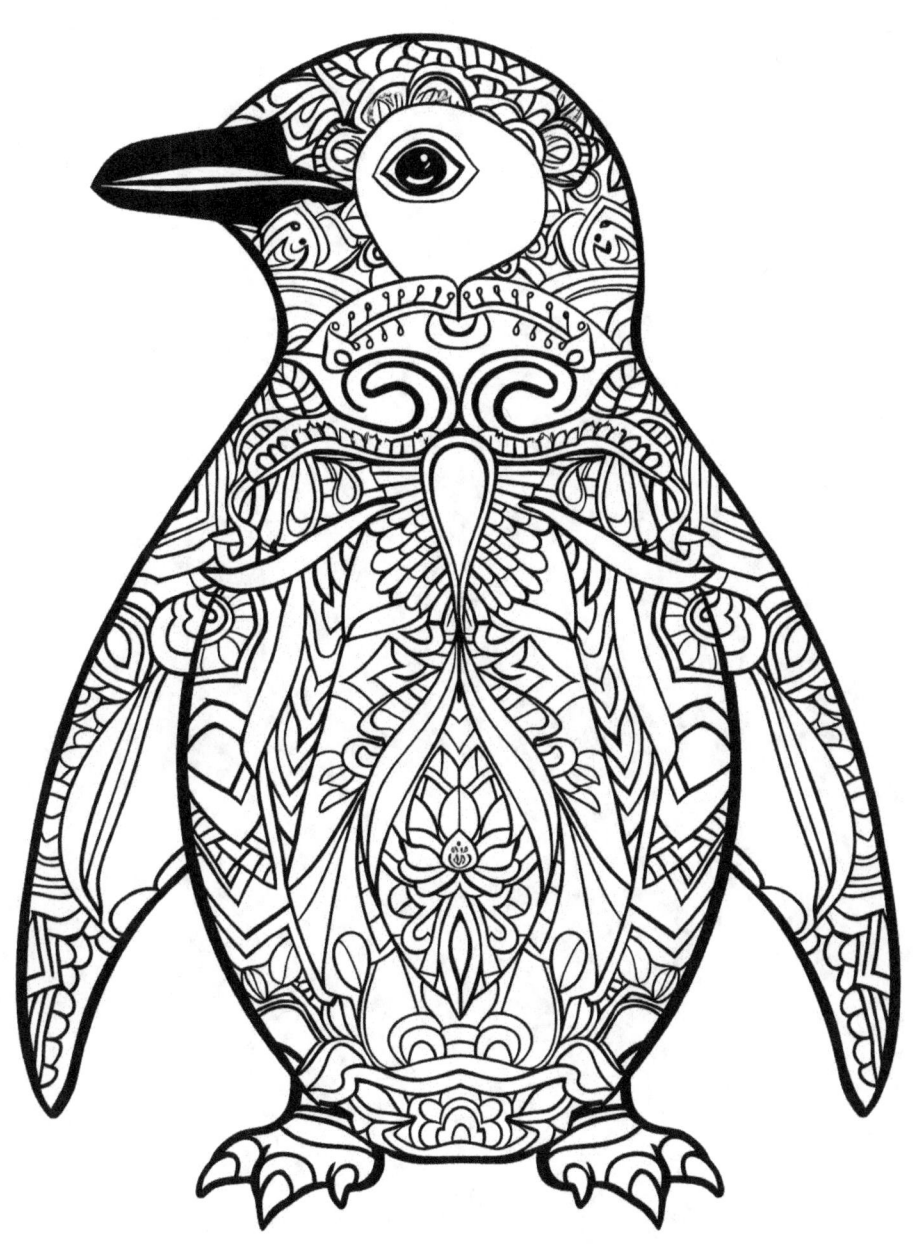

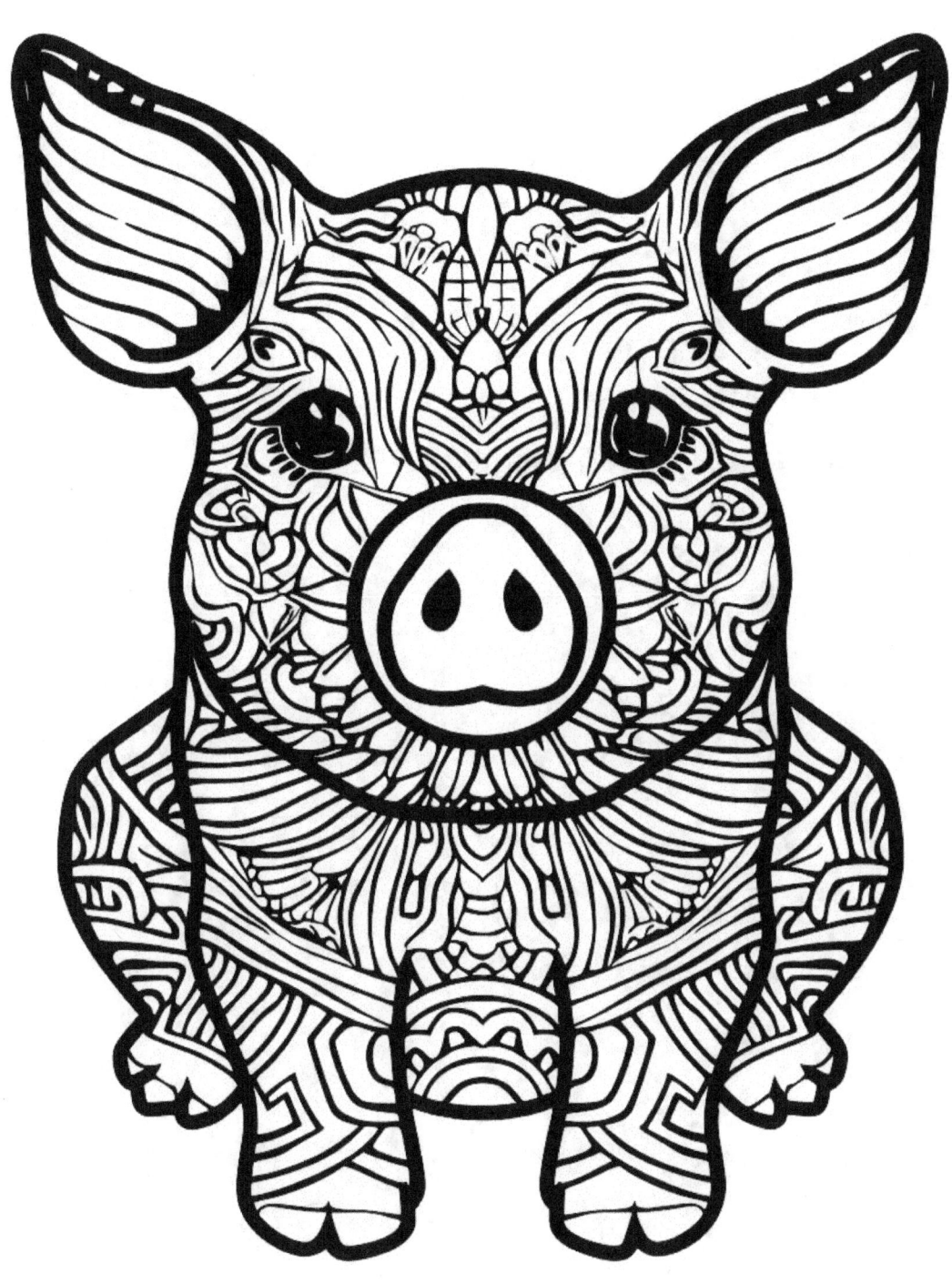

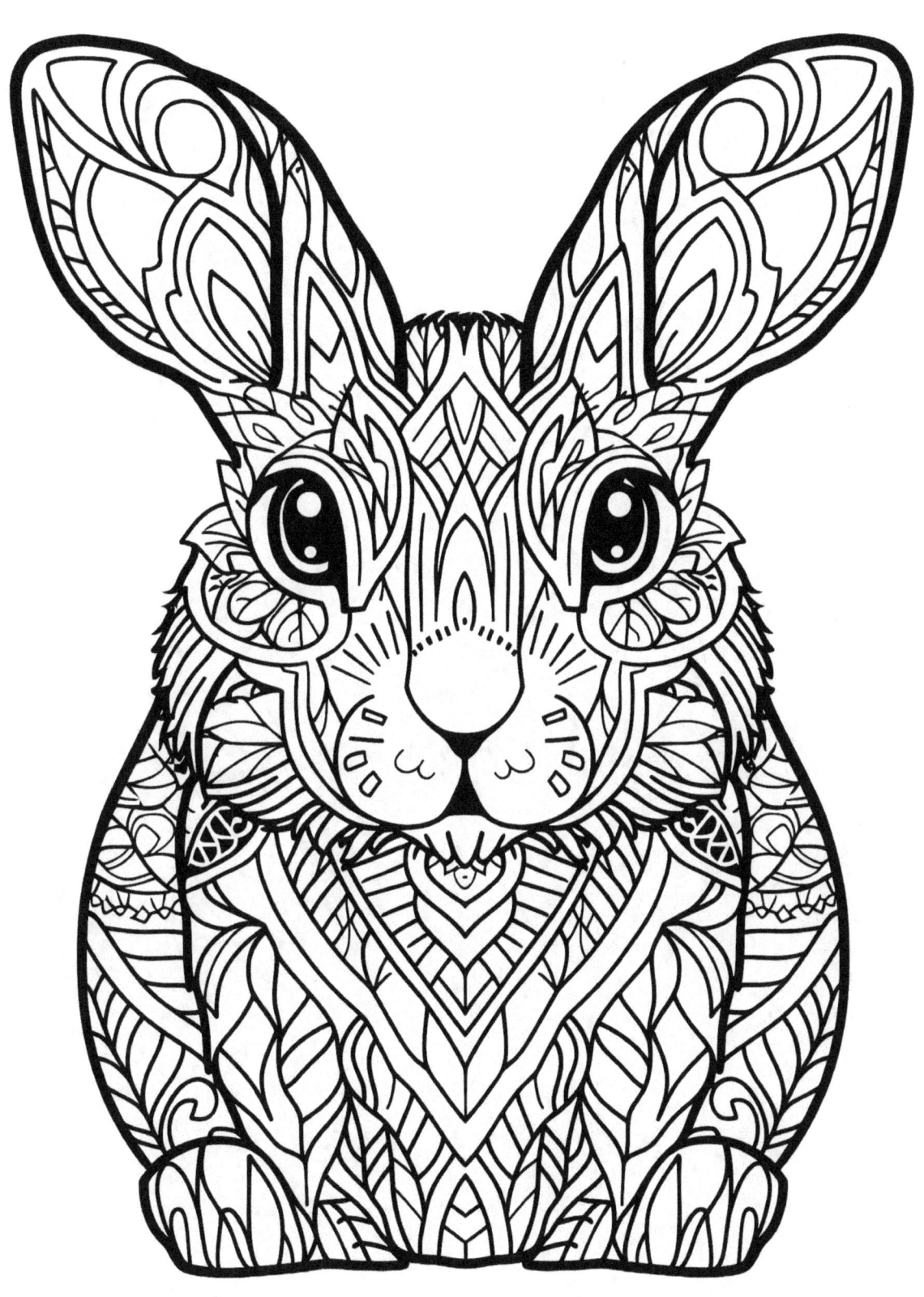

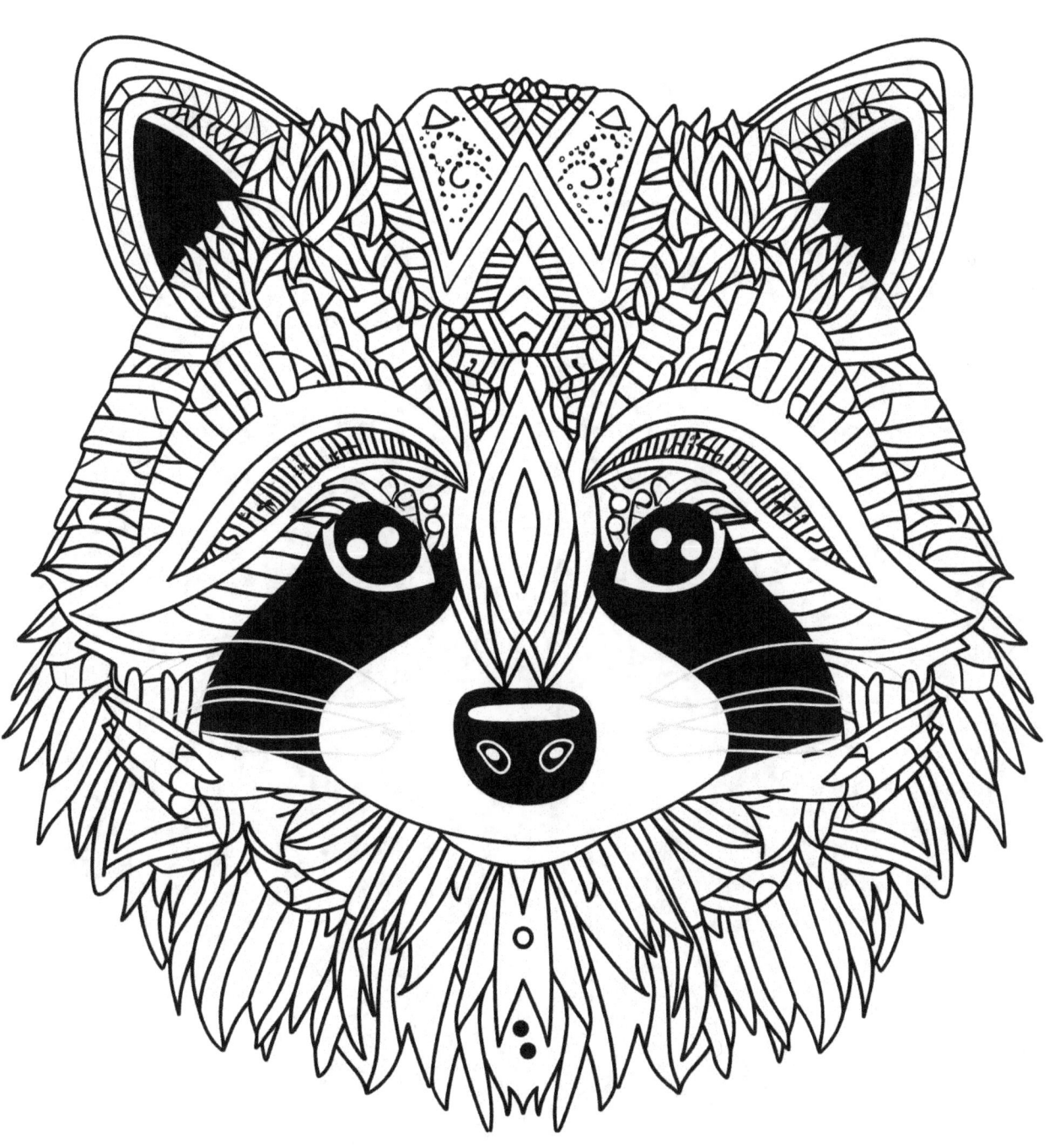

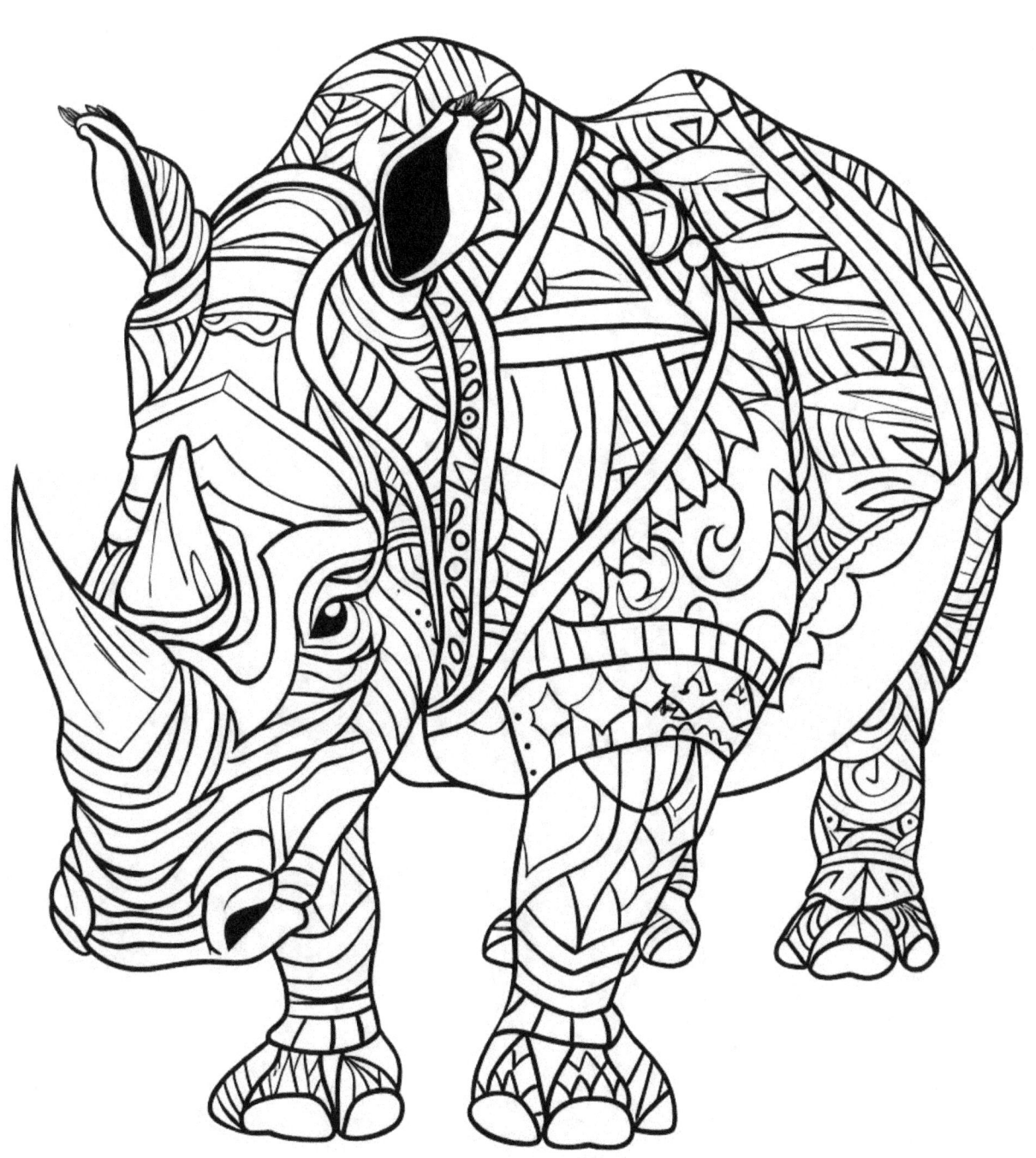

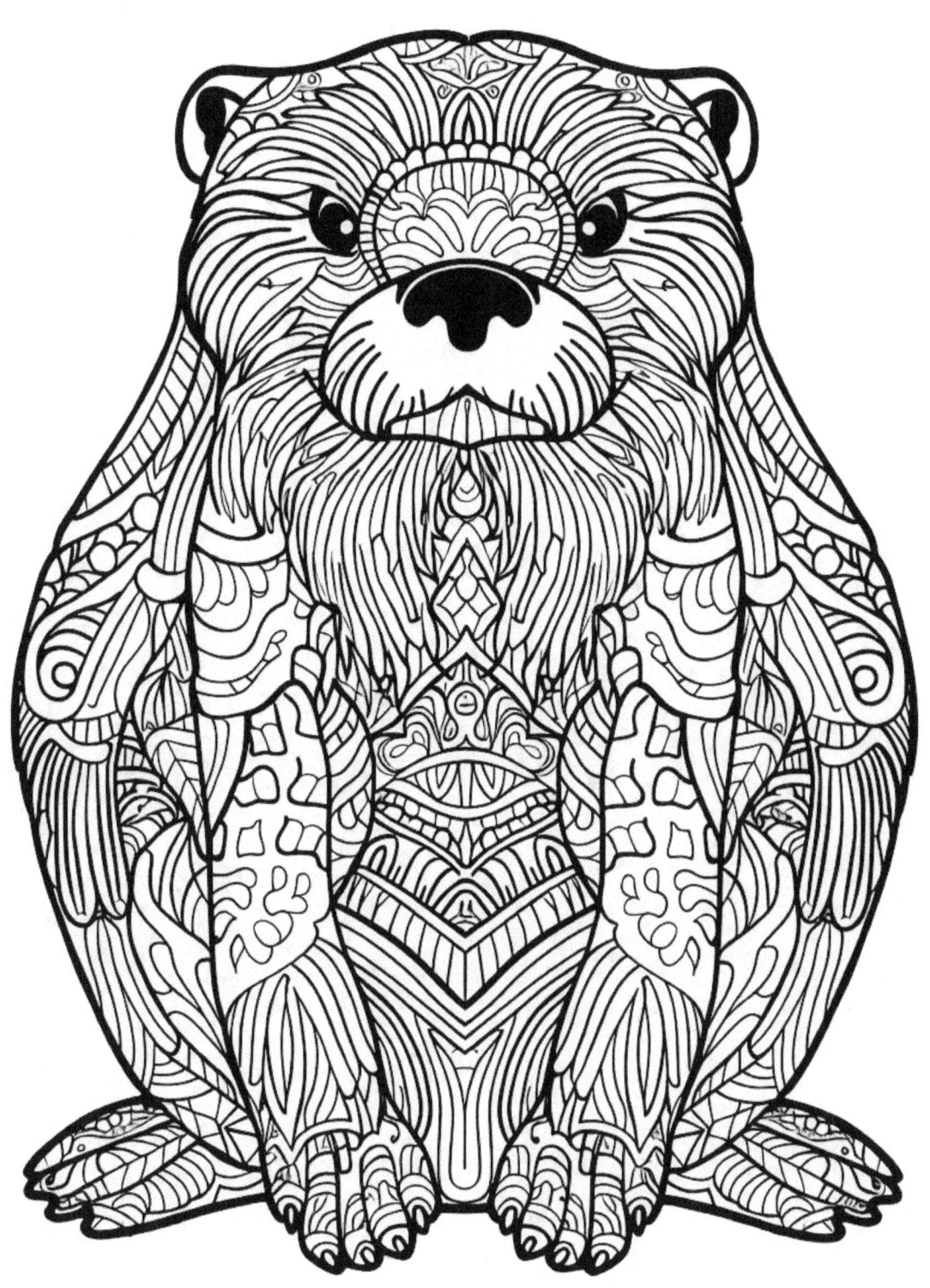

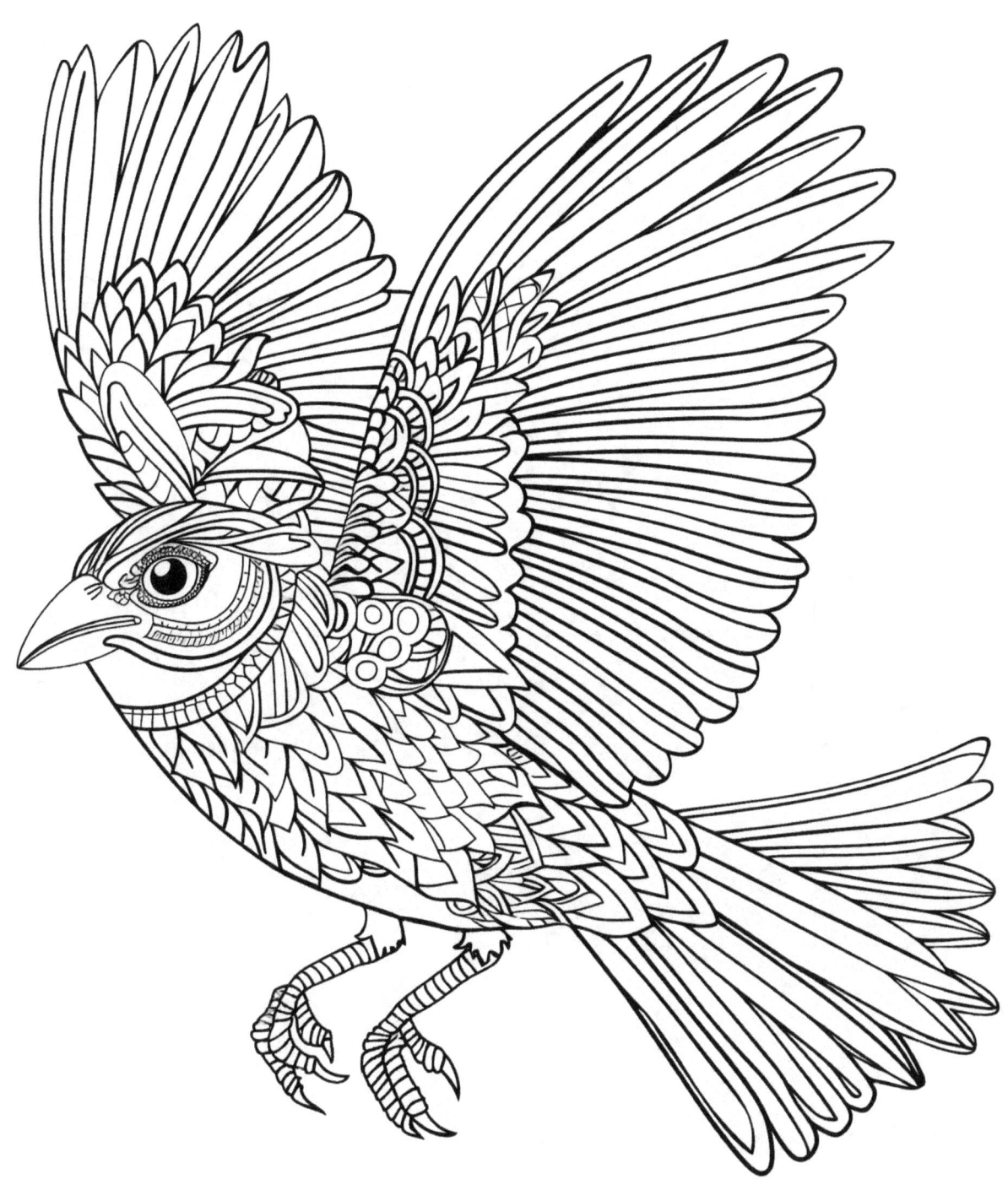

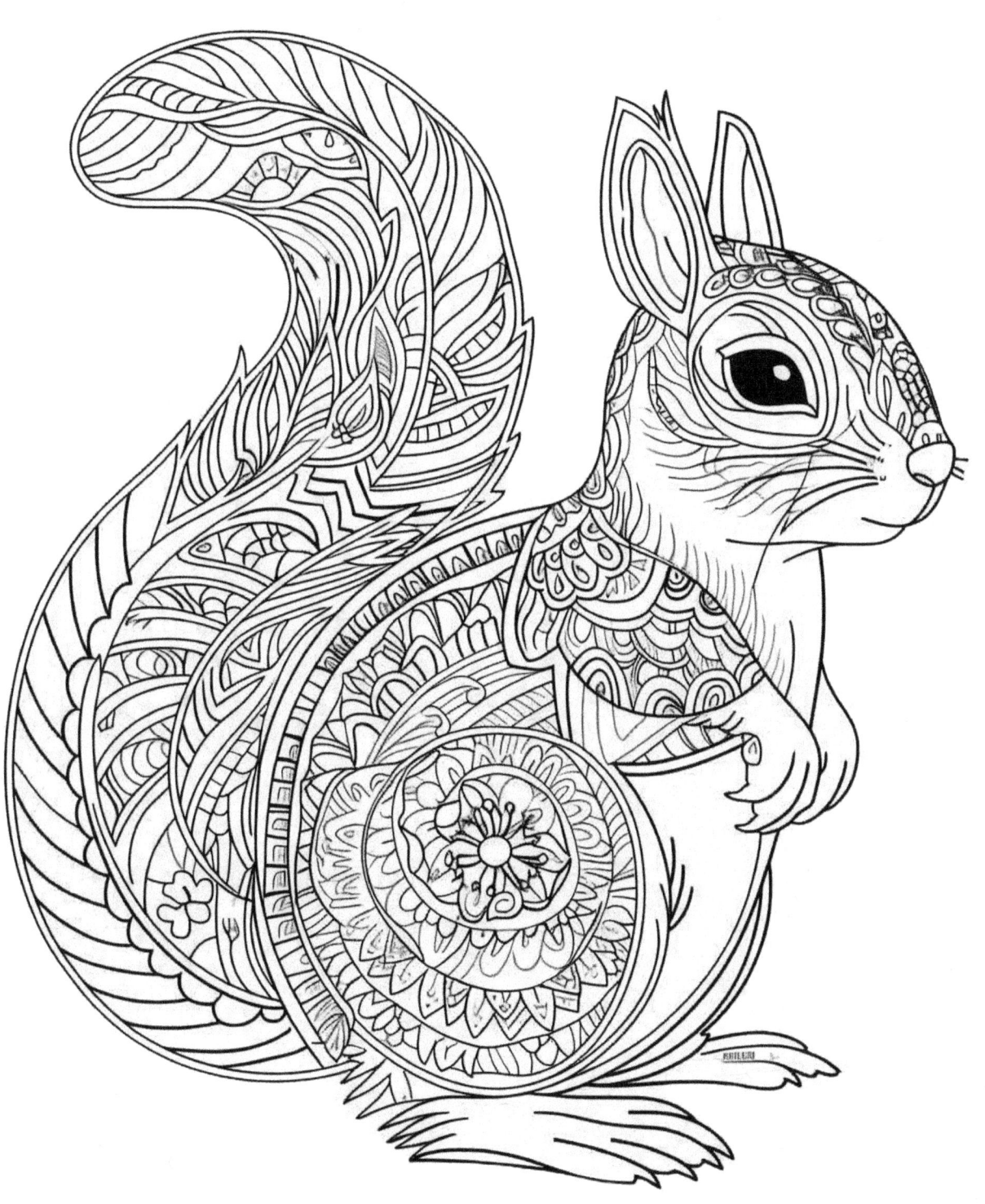

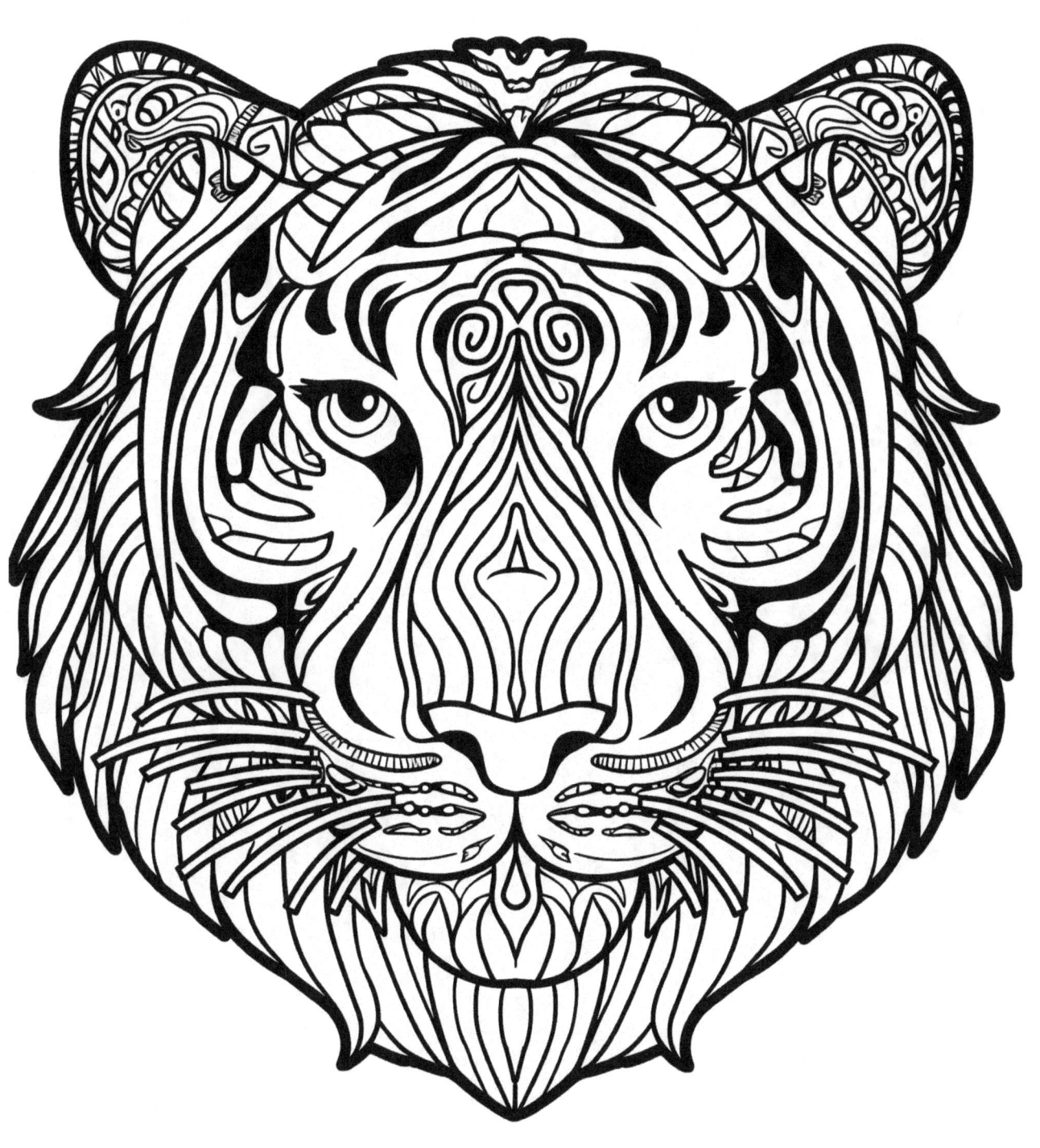

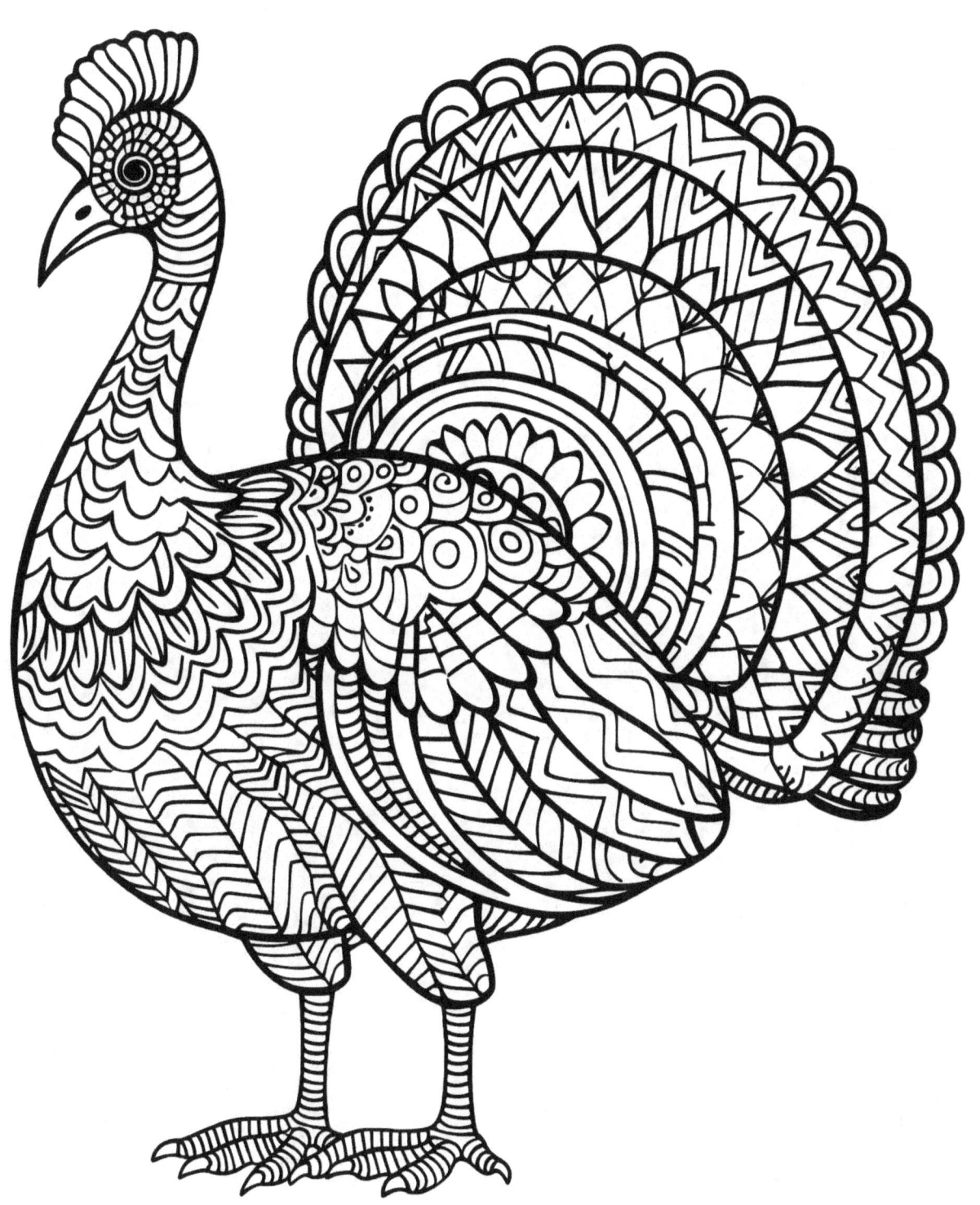

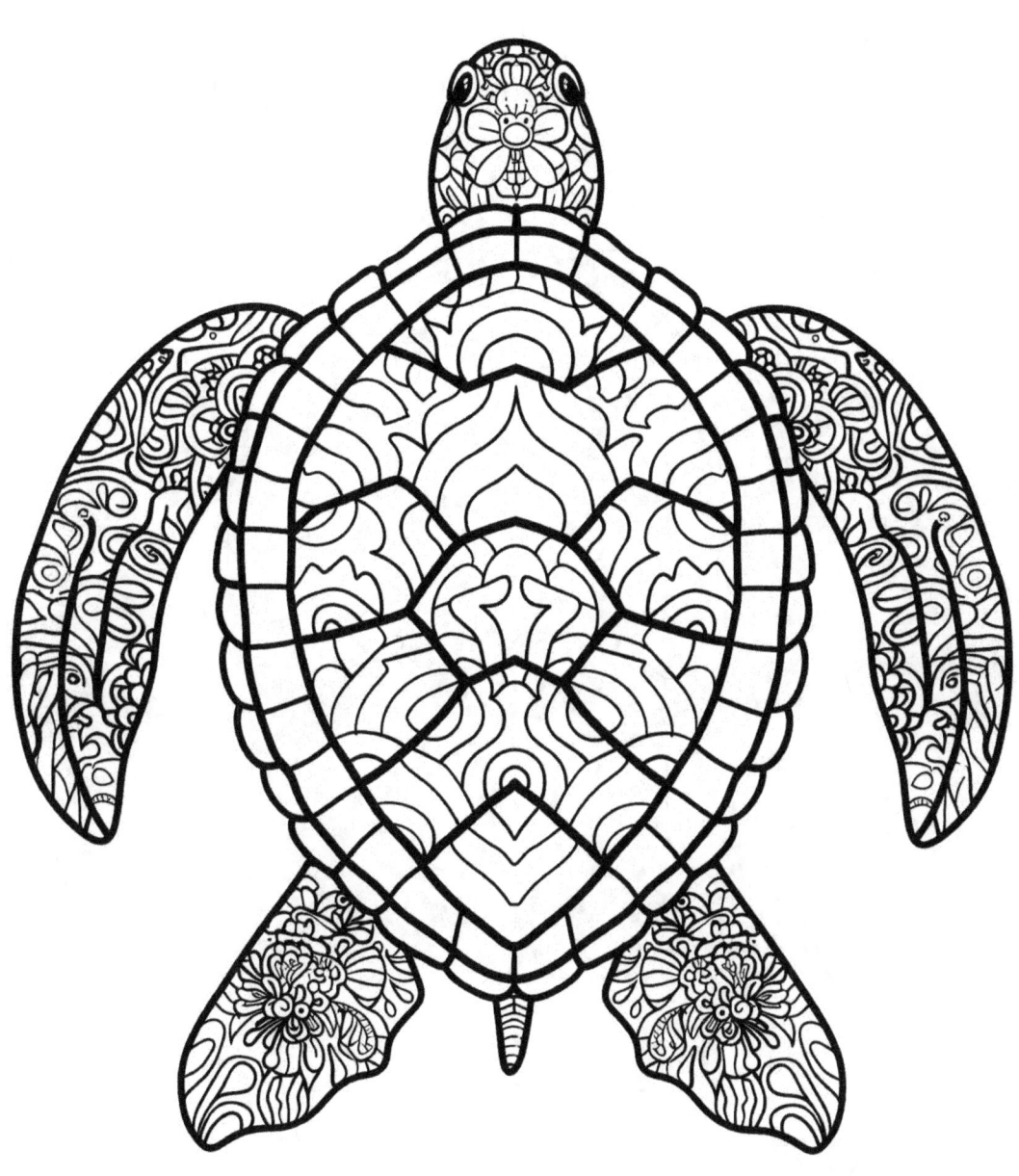

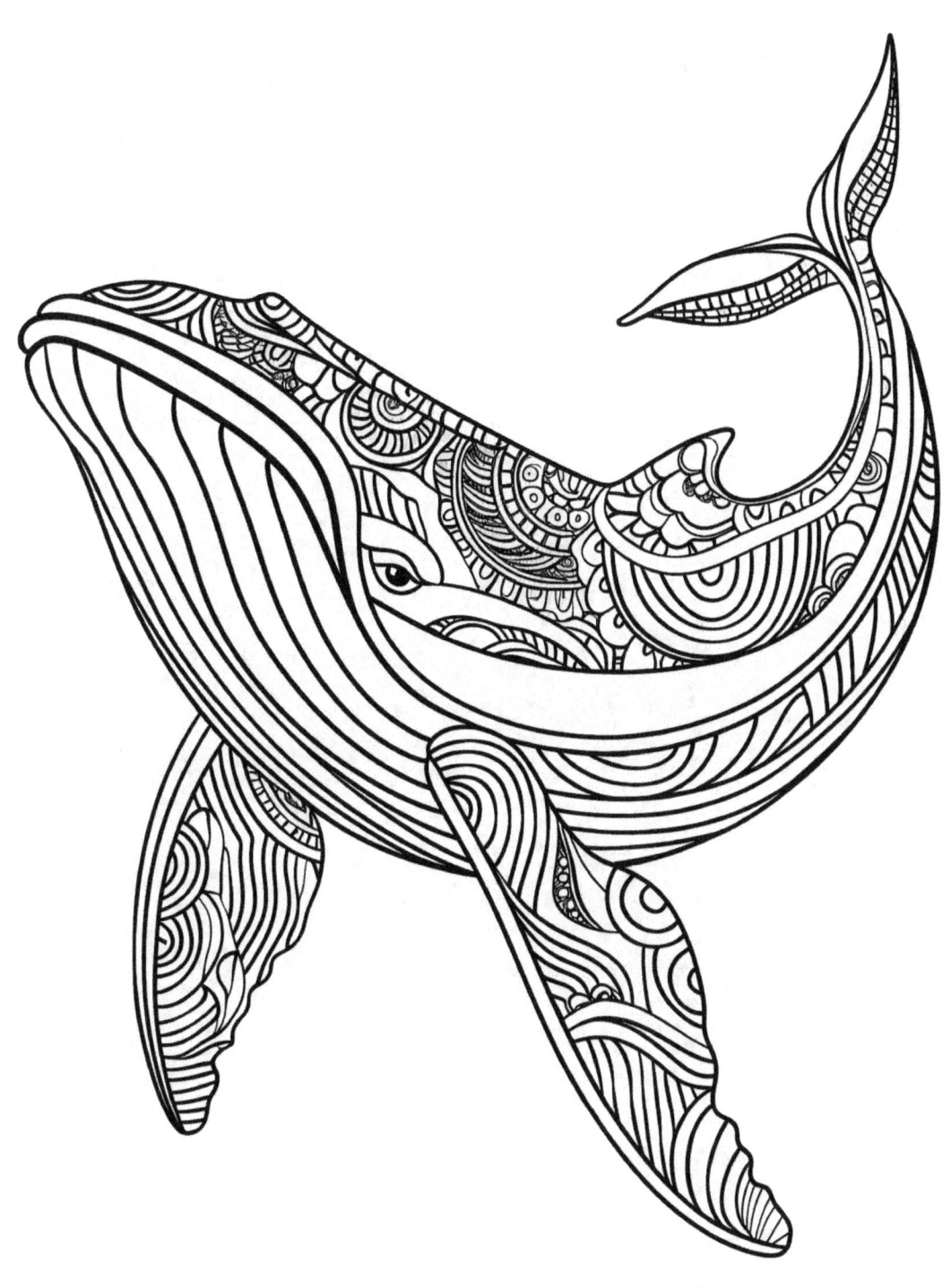

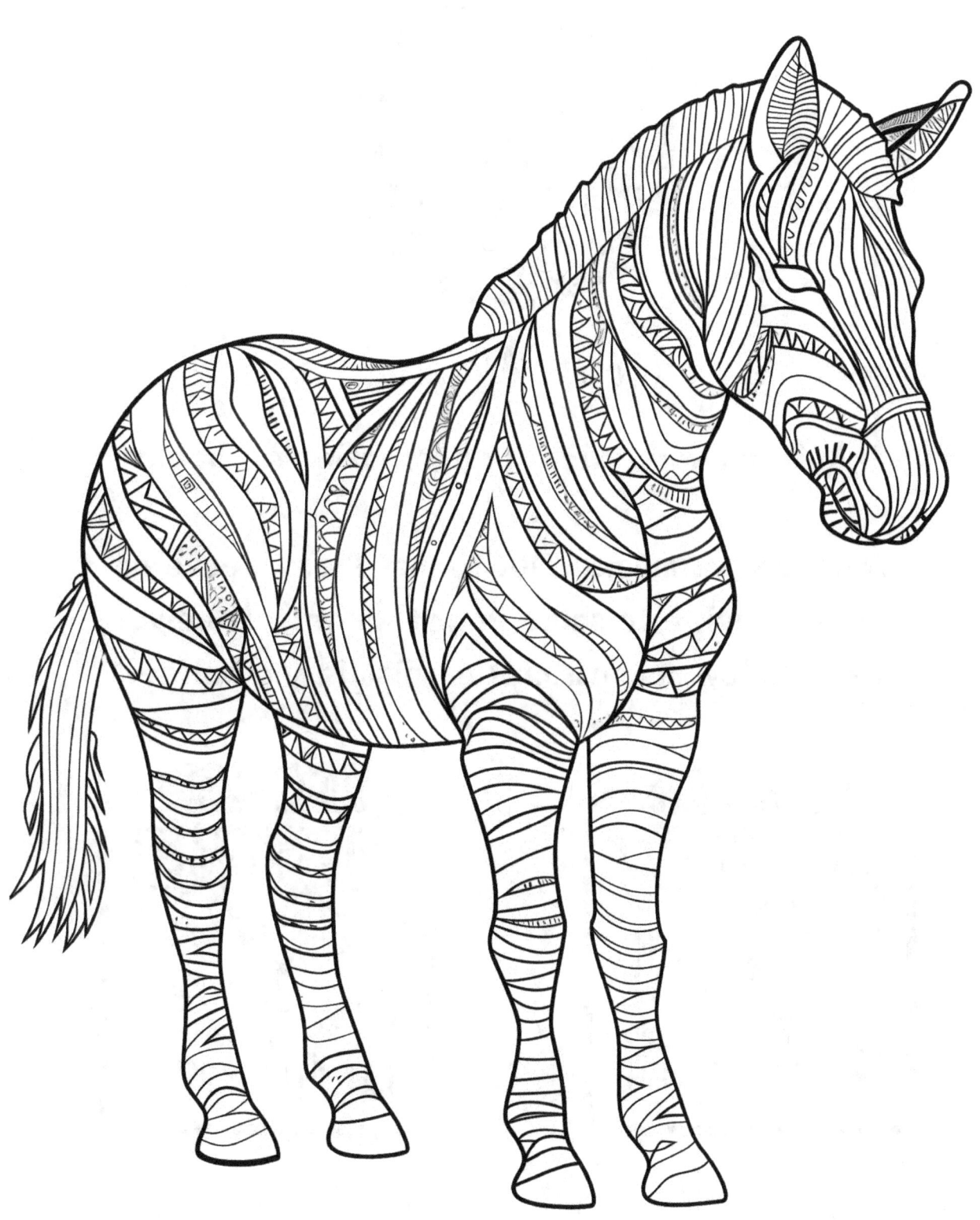

Please rate this book!

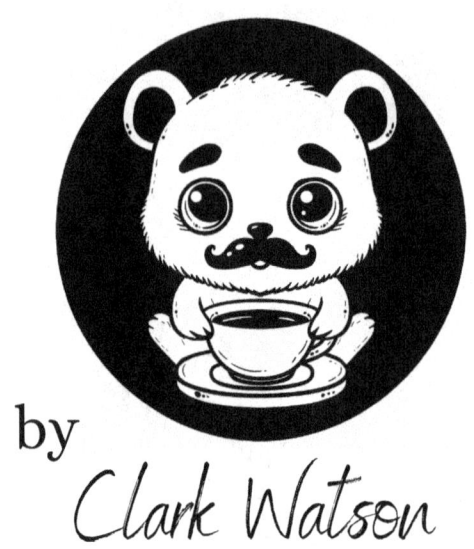

by

Clark Watson

Thank you very much for purchasing my book!

Your support means a lot to me. Please leave an honest review to share your thoughts. It helps me to follow my passion for animals and coffee.

REVIEW PAGE

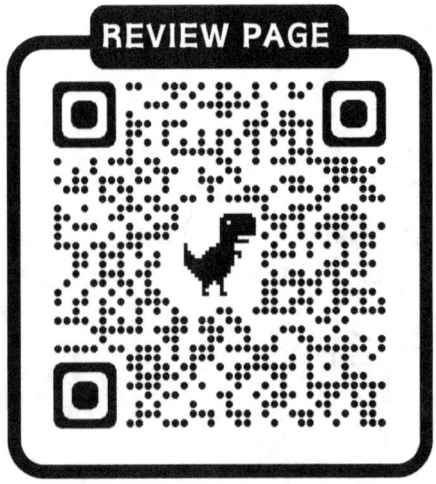

AUTHOR PAGE